THE SECRETS OF WRITING

James Hudnall

The Secrets of Writing

James Hudnall

thehud.com

fortanmedia.com

Also by James Hudnall

Hell's Reward

Espers: The Storm

Espers: Interface

Espers: Undertow

Espers: Crossfire

Chiller

2 To the Chest

Streets

The Age of Heroes

The Psycho

Sinking

Blue Cat

Devastator

Shut Up And Die

Aftermath

For David Lloyd, friend and first collaborator.
Thanks for everything.

Special thanks:

Todd Mulrooney for the cover.

Maya Eilam (mayaeilam.com) for the Story Shape
infographics.

Batton Lash (supernaturallaw.com) for the Section
illustrations.

Kurt Vonnegut for Story Shape theory.

1

FOREWORD

When I sat down to write this thing I became possessed. I thought about it every waking moment. I even had dreams about this book. It really took over my life. Since I was a kid I wanted to be a writer. I didn't become one until I was 28 with my first comic, Espers. As I became more experienced, the theory and practice of this art form became more interesting to me. I became fascinated with exploring the form in other media like books and film.

Then I set this book aside, for almost 20 years. I came back to it now and again, but I finally felt it was time to finish it. So I did.

Since I started out as a comics writer there will be a lot of references to comics. But this book is for writing in general. Most of my references are to films because that is what most people have been exposed to. Writing is writing. There are different expectations from different media. Each as its strengths and weaknesses, but the principles of writing are the same.

My goal was to create a comprehensive, easy to

understand, book on writing in general, with a slant toward the comics industry. You can use the principles outlined in this book to write comics, novels, movies, plays, you name it. I've tried to dissect and analyze every aspect of writing and storytelling I could think of. I went back and read a whole stack of books to refresh my understanding of other people's theories so I wouldn't leave anything out.

I've tried to make this book simple by keeping the terminology simple. Terms like Protagonist and Antagonist have become Hero and Villain. I avoid "politically correct" terminology and refer to generic characters as "he". "Audience" was used instead of "Reader" because you're not just writing to one person but many. Hopefully, many people will experience what you write. They're your audience.

Occasionally I'll discuss books or comics, but again, I'll stick to popular work so you'll have an easy time finding it if you haven't read it.

Hopefully, you'll find this book as useful as I have. Putting my thoughts in order and brushing up on text books has given me a lot of fresh insights. You're never too old, or too experienced, to learn new things. Sometimes you also need to refresh your knowledge.

No one, no matter who they are, is above learning new tricks.

Experience is important, but not always enough. You can learn a lot by doing, but some new tricks might evade you. That's why it's wise to keep abreast of all the literary journals and theories out there. And talk to other writers. Swap notes. It's good for you!

You may find it annoying that certain maxims are repeated over and over again in this book. It's because these principles need to be permanently etched in your mind. You need to remember these things better than any of the Ten Commandments. But, while everything in here is true, there are always exceptions. Consider the following to be the basics and take it from there.

Breaking rules is a creative choice. But first you need to learn them or you're an amateur,

REMEMBER: There are no "rules" to writing, only "principles".

THE BASICS

"It isn't the job of the artist to give the audience what the audience wants. It's the job of the artist to give audience what they need."
Alan Moore

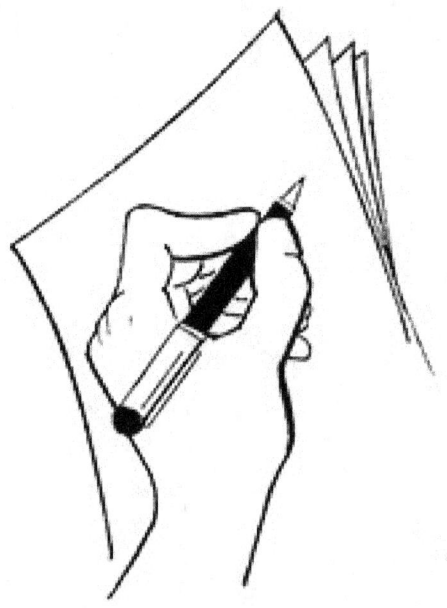

SO YOU WANT TO BE A WRITER

A lot of people say they want to be a writer. A lot of people say they *plan* to be a writer. A lot of people dream of being a writer.

Writers write. They don't talk about it. They don't dream about it. They do it. It's the only way you will ever be a writer. By doing.

The only way to get good is to do more writing. And never stop trying to learn. Never stop watching plays, movies and shows if that interests you, to study the techniques and structure. Never stop reading comics or books to learn from them. Books especially, because there is where things can get a lot more dense and magical. All forms of writing have their unique advantages and disadvantages over the other. It would be wrong to decide one medium is inferior to the other because they all require the same fundamentals. There is worthless drek in all media so none is without its share of crap. But all media has its classics as well. I have worked mainly in comics in my career but have transitioned to prose and film. You can do it all. But you have to write.

A big mistake many creative people make is getting upset by other people's success. It's none of your business. Your career is *your* business and if it's suffering then stop wasting your time obsessing about other people's careers. It's a waste of energy. Energy and time better spent.

Spend it creating.

Your biggest enemy will be one person. That person is you. You will hold yourself back more than anyone. You may think that's not true but you're the one you has to do the hard work.. You're the one who has to stop procrastinating and making excuses. You are the one who gets lazy and slacks off or plays video games or does drugs instead of producing a masterpiece.

You are the only one stopping you. So defeat your weaknesses. Get fit in the head and focus.

Here's the good news. It has never been a better time to be a writer because you can do it more easily than at any time in history. You don't need a publisher anymore. You don't need anyone's permission. There are all sorts of new places to publish your work no matter what form it takes. All you have to do is create it.

Of course, there will be work to do after that called promotion. That will be harder than writing your work. But here's the great thing about being a writer. Once you finish something it will exist as long as you keep it alive in some form. Once it's published. Once it's on the cloud or in print, it exists and will exist for a long time. How long depends on may things, but the beauty is, you can write something when you're young and still make money off it when you're old.

But you have to write it first. And that goes back to what I said above. Only you can stop you. So don't stop yourself.

You want to be a writer? Then write something.

This book is here to help you. I try to give you all the tools you need to do the job.

But it's up to you to after that.

Write!

WHAT IS A STORY

We are, by nature, a creative animal. We're driven to make our mark on the world in some fashion, beyond our need to survive. Some people satisfy their creativity in the business world. Some satisfy it with music or dance. We're going to focus on that most ancient of trades...storytelling.

Mankind, as we know it, has been on earth for at least 40,000 years. We can safely assume that somewhere in the midst of that time, people started telling stories. It all probably originated around the campfire when we lived in caves and hunted with flint spears. Stories began as one hunter bragged about some saber-tooth he killed, or a fish that got away. As people's tastes became more sophisticated, the demands on a story grew. There needed to be more at stake, more interesting things happening, and that required technique.

We don't know when people first started formulating story technique, but we know from recorded history that they began doing it in Ancient Greece, about 2,500 years ago. The first known plays were performed there, in honor of the god Dionysius. Stories were acted out with pantomime and dialog before a live audience. The actors wore masks depicting the mood of the character. Writers quickly saw the need for improving their craft when actors started speaking their lines. Before then, stories were told by one performer who was usually the guy who made them up, or they were written on stone tablets where only those with the skill to read could appreciate them. Now you had a whole new art form where flaws in a story became more brutally apparent.

The Greek philosopher Aristotle was one of the first to write a treatise on the subject of crafting an effective tale. In "De Poetica" he laid the groundwork for the theory we now know as *Story Structure.*

Story Structure is the foundation upon which all stories are built. It is the framework that holds a story together. You cannot write a story without employing it. However, if you don't understand the principles of story structure, you can easily make a mess. This is one reason why so many stories out there are bad. The authors of those narratives didn't employ the principles of structure appropriately.

It's kind of like that old biblical parable about the man who built his house on the sand, while another built his house on stony earth. The house built on the beach got destroyed because the foundation was built on unstable ground. The same thing happens to a story built with a poor structure. It falls apart.

The last thing any good writer wants is to spend days, months, or years on something that's ultimately weak. Aside from the blow to your self esteem and the rejection of the public, it doesn't do your career a whole lot of good.

There is a big problem with structure however. It's such a vast and complex subject, many people mistakenly think of it as a formula. Aristotle and some of the theorists who followed didn't help matters by actually defining the formula, as they saw it, rather than revealing structure as a series of principles, which is what it is. Think of it as a form, rather than a formula. Structure is the form your story takes.

Formula writers mistakenly follow the notion that plot twists have to occur on a certain page, characters must be introduced a precise way, etc. We'll get into that later on. But. by dogmatically following these formulas, they end up creating predictable, by-the-numbers plots that don't do a whole lot to satisfy the audience. You can see this kind of writing in many movies, TV shows, novels, comics, et al.

Structure is a theory, like numbers theory in math or music theory in music. The theory allows us to understand and affect things the way we would like. It provides a whole spectrum of methods to get from point A to point B. You don't have to follow any specific path to get to where you want to go. You just need to understand the general rules and apply them as you see fit.

REMEMBER: Story structure is a series of principles. It's *not* a formula.

MEANING MAKES A STORY

"My task, which I am trying to achieve is, by the power of the written word, to make you hear, to make you feel - it is, before all, to make you see."
Joseph Conrad

Theodore Sturgeon was a classic science fiction writer who coined what has come to be known as "Sturgeon's Law". It goes something like this: "90% of everything is crap."

He's pretty much correct, but crap sells sometimes. The question is, do you want to produce crap? Because stories like that are quickly forgotten whether they sell or not. And let's be frank, most writers will have to deal with rejection. Crap is nothing to aspire to. It's worthless for a reason.

You want to feel good about your work. There's something to be said for the theory that art is therapy. We suffer though our art but in the end we produce meaning and beauty.

There is one thing that lifts good stories above the drek. What separates the wheat from the chaff and that is meaning. A good story has a point. It has something to say. It sheds light on the human condition or the darkness in men's souls. It says something no one is willing to say. It reveals painful truths about life or it answers questions people are always seeking answers too.

Junk fiction does none of that. It's empty calories. But great stories last through the ages. The Iliad and the Odyssey are two of the greatest stories ever told. They have been been around for thousands of years. Charles Dickens and Mark Twain are still being read over 100 years after they died. Victor Hugo, Cervantes, Tolstoy, there are a whole lot of dead writers who are still required reading in school. What separates them from the mountain of forgotten books? I'll tell you.

They revealed some truth in their stories that still resonates with people to this day. Great stories stay with you by providing meaning. By providing context for things we often find elusive. But more importantly, they help fill in the gaps in that crazy puzzle we call life.

Fiction was invented to answer questions people had no answers for. The early stories answered questions like, why are there storms or death, with myths about the gods. Later fiction dealt with other questions on society, injustice, poverty, things people still think about today and no one has a satisfying solution. But fiction can at least make sense of the senselessness of our existence. People respond to cause and effect. Our mind is trained to understand things by seeking patterns. A good story weaves those patterns together in such a way that a truth becomes revealed. Answers where none were before.

Story structure is a method of making the pattern take shape. But to understand this better, we can reverse engineer the story so the structure is revealed in a way that makes sense in a simple way. The famous author Kurt Vonnegut (Slaughterhouse Nine, Breakfast of Champions) wrote a thesis on the shape of stories that illustrates what we're talking about. He is basically showing how the structure of a story can be visually represented. Here are a few of his examples.

Story shape can be summed up as simply at the chart above. A story has two states, positive and negative, which is where your characters will find themselves at any point in the story. Since time as a human experience is linear, and since, for the sake of this example, we'll deal with the classical structure, time is where the story starts and ends. It separates the events of the story in one line. The positive side is everything north of the time line, the negative is south of the line.

Stories start either positive or negative. Events will go one a certain direction until there us a incident that makes it switch gears. In this simple example you see a character has all kinds of good things happen to them at the start of the story then half way something changes their fortune and it gets dark. It ends up one the other side of the line and then only starts to climb back toward the end. This is not a typical story, as we will explain later, but it gives you and idea of the shape.

Things happen in the plot in the wavy area which is really a one dimensional line that goes up and down depending on where things are in the story. For the purposes of this discussion, we show plot events happening in this area so you can imagine them by way of example.

Our first example is two classic story plot that are also some of the most commonly used. You can see from the illustration, they are very similar

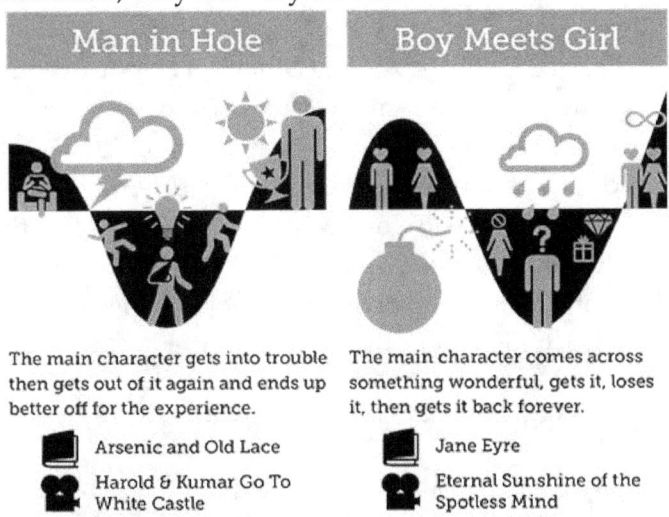

Man in Hole

The main character gets into trouble then gets out of it again and ends up better off for the experience.

📖 Arsenic and Old Lace

🎬 Harold & Kumar Go To White Castle

Boy Meets Girl

The main character comes across something wonderful, gets it, loses it, then gets it back forever.

📖 Jane Eyre

🎬 Eternal Sunshine of the Spotless Mind

The Man in Hole is a classic story that is often used in comedy. A character or characters have their lives upturned. They find themselves in a bad place. And then work to get back on top. It's simple and it has worked in so many different plots you would be amazed. Almost every major comedy in modern time is a variation on this classic. Think about it.

Boy Meets Girl is the basis of just about every romance ever written. Two people meet. They are attracted to each other but they have differences. Things turn sour and get complicated. One of them keeps trying to win the other over, or they bond through shared suffering of some kind. This leads to things improving as conflicts are resolved and they end up happily in love.

What they have in common is they usually start with things going well for the main characters, but then events turn sour. There is a point where events lead to a series of hardships and trials that the characters have to overcome to get their lives back on track or to cheat death. Once they do, the story ends with them rewarded with success of some kind.

The original *Star Wars: A New Hope* is a classic example of what is known as the romance story. Innocents are thrown into a war, they go through all sorts of death defying adventures until they are rewarded with great success. That same basic story was also used in *Conan the Barbarian, Guardians of the Galaxy, The Lord of the Rings* and a host of others. In the course of those stories the main characters learned something about themselves that was a revelation to them.

Here are a couple more, complex examples.

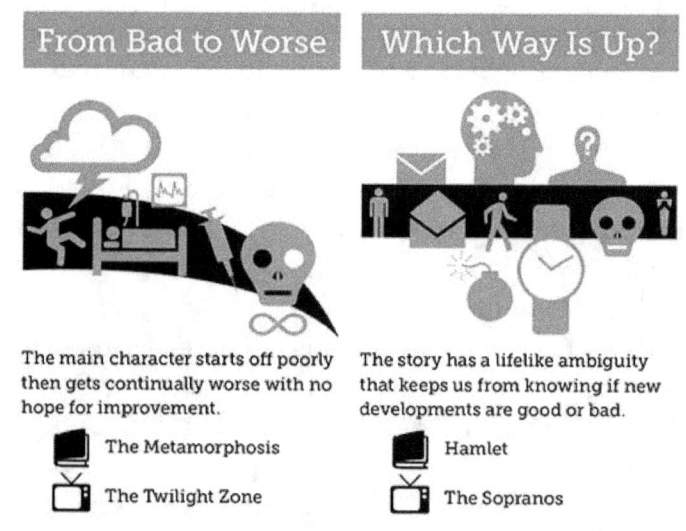

The main character starts off poorly then gets continually worse with no hope for improvement.

The Metamorphosis

The Twilight Zone

The story has a lifelike ambiguity that keeps us from knowing if new developments are good or bad.

Hamlet

The Sopranos

Here we see a Fall type story where someone starts off well, but a series of bad events put them in a negative state at the conclusion. They give the example of Franz Kafka's *Metamorphosis* where a man awakes to find himself a large cockroach. The other example, *The Twilight Zone* which often had stories with negative endings. This is a one way trip through the story values discussed later on.

By contrast, the Which Way is Up pattern is more random. In stories like that it's hard to tell who's the hero or the villain, the results are often ironic.

We derive meaning from stories based on a lot of factors which we will discuss in this book. But I wanted to talk about shapes so you can see how events shape the outcome and the feel of the piece.

REMEMBER: People want to find meaning in your work, not just entertainment.

Infographics: Maya Eilam (mayaeilam.com)

STORY

This is a subject many writers disagree on. The difference between a plot and a story has been argued since Aristotle stirred things up back in Old Athens. For the record, I'm going to take the side of writers like George Bernard Shaw who said: "There are only two stories. 'Cinderella' and 'Jack and the Beanstalk.'"

Translation: "Boy Meets Girl" and "The Hero on a Quest".

However, I part company with Mr. Shaw on the number of stories. I really think there is only *one* story. The Hero on a Quest. Because Boy Meets Girl is about one or more characters questing for an object of desire. Love.

Man Vs Nature is often quoted as another basic story. But that story is about a hero questing for peace and quiet, or better weather. When you really think about it, all stories are about characters trying to get something. Either an abstract thing like peace of mind, or a material object, like a bag of money.

We all want something. That is one thing that will be a human constant. Desire.

Every story is about someone wanting something and what they have to do to get it. They way not *know* they want it, but they will by the story's end.

The definition of "quest" is: to seek for something, or a mission to perform a goal. Therefore, we find many completely different plots all end up with the same basic story. Examples:

JURASSIC PARK: Scientists seek to survive when monsters get loose.

STAR WARS: A young man seeks justice in a troubled

universe.

JAWS: The sheriff of a beach town goes on a mission to kill a monster.

THE GODFATHER: A young man seeks to create order in a troubled world.

THE WIZARD OF OZ: A young girl searches for home when she is lost.

GONE WITH THE WIND: A young woman seeks love in a troubled world.

CITIZEN KANE: A reporter seeks for the secret to "Rosebud"

FORREST GUMP: A mentally disabled man seeks for love in a troubled world.

SCHINDLER'S LIST: A Nazi seeks to save Jews from injustice.

BATMAN: A hero seeks to create justice in a troubled world.

As you can see, in all these stories we have a character, or characters, seeking to obtain something or achieve a goal. They are all heroes on a quest.

Boil down any story and you end up with this formula: A>B<C

A (the hero) wants C (the Object of Desire) and B (the conflict/villain) stands in the way.

Just as there is only one basic story, there are only three possible endings to a story. Success, failure, or both at the same time. But we'll get to that in a later chapter.

If you understand there is only one kind of story, it makes it a lot easier to focus on your goals. You now know that in every story, your hero is trying to achieve something. You have to decide what that is. It doesn't have to be limited to one goal, as we will discuss later, there are usually multiple goals in a story, but they are usually part and parcel of the same thing.

We are all trying to get something. That is what life is about. The second we are born, we want. Food, sex, drugs, money, power, clothes, shelter, happiness, love, revenge, you name it. We are all motivated by desire. We are creatures of need. Hunger is something everyone can relate to. Stories satisfy us when we can identify with a Hero and his desires, even if we disagree with his motives or methods.

To make your story unique, you elaborate on the one story in a way the Audience has either never seen, or never expected. But it has to be in a manner they will agree with and enjoy.

Therein lies the rub.

REMEMBER: Every story is about "A" wanting "C" and "B" stands in the way.

PLOT

If a story is about something, how characters come together in conflict over a thing they desire, for example. Then a plot is the mechanics of how it happens.

It deals with the events, or scenes, that make up the parts of the story.

When you hear a plot has holes it means they forgot to explain some obvious things. They forgot to show something that explains context or something that would make a scene believable.

It's a common problem in a lot of stories, which is why we're going to show you how to avoid that.

Again, there is only one story, but an infinite variety of plots. Plots are like a machine. You start with a bunch of parts, which are the story elements, and put them together until the thing works. The purpose of this machine is to arouse the Audience's expectations. To excite them.

Plots come in two levels. There is the basic plot, or synopsis, which is the plot boiled down to a paragraph. And there's the expanded plot, or the outline, which is the sequence of events around which a story is decorated and embellished. The plot's plot, if you will.

A plot is what many people call a story. And it's not wrong to call it a story. Every plot is a story. It's merely a story dressed up as a plot. It gets confusing when writers argue the difference between plot and story. My definition keeps things simple. Why get complicated?

Story is the bottle. Plot is the wine. Bad wine is sour. Good wine is fine. Make your plots fine wine.

In case you're confused by the above ramble, I'll explain it another way. A plot is the story blown up and embellished with events, characters, and scenes. Think of the story as an evergreen and the plot as all the blinking lights, tinsel, and colored glass balls needed to turn that bland evergreen into a Christmas tree.

Every Christmas tree is unique, because the size of the tree can be large or small, the choice of decorations are as varied as the tastes of the decorators. But everyone knows it's a Christmas tree when they see it. A plot, like a Christmas tree, will be as unique as the imagination of the writer can make it.

The decorations are the characters, scenes, and techniques used to make the story more exciting. Once they're all in place you have a plot.

The Types of Plot

In *classic* story structure, often plots take one of two basic forms:

The Progressive Version is where the conflict keeps getting more and more intense for the hero as the story progresses until he reaches a point of no return. This is the crisis of the story where the whole outcome is determined. Examples: DIE HARD, NORTH BY NORTHWEST, STAR WARS.

The Sequential Version is where the hero has a series of adventures that each advance the story, explore the premise, and lead us to an inevitable conclusion. This form is hard to pull off and maintain direction. Examples are: FORREST GUMP, HUCKLEBERRY FINN, THE ODYSSEY

The Plot Diagram

Just as a story has a shape, so do plots. They are often referred to as plot diagrams. The plot diagram can come in many different forms, as you'd expect but they basically follow a certain shape. We will delve into that in the next part. The story shapes we discussed previously are basically the same as the plot diagram except the diagram gets into more finer points as we will discuss shortly.

REMEMBER: There is only one story, but a zillion plots.

STORY STRUCTURE

Plots are built like a house on the foundation called story structure. Structure is the materials that the plot is made from.

There are three basic types of structure. Classical, Minimalist, and Surreal. This book focuses on Classical Structure which is the most popular form with Audiences. But it's important to understand the other two so you can decide if you want to play with them.

CLASSICAL: This structure is the one most widely used in fiction, especially in film. It has proved to be the structure that creates the greatest emotional response in an audience. We have thousands of years of fiction to prove it. Classical story structure means change for the characters. They don't come away from the story without their lives being affected in some way. All the questions in the story are answered. All emotions raised are satisfied. In Classical structure the emphasis is mainly on external conflict and causality. The Hero is proactive. The time chronology in the story is usually linear. There is a consistent reality. Time also flows in a way that is close to what people are used to. Even if it jumps ahead, it will tend to be moving forward. Flashbacks are clearly defined as something from the past like a memory. In other words, it's straightforward, easy to follow and not confusing in any way. What is what most people prefer a story to be.

MINIMALIST: This form of deals with stories that do not affect change in the characters lives. They come away at the end the same as when they started. These stories usually have open endings, unresolved climaxes. Some of the questions in the story get answered, but some are left for the audience to think about. The emphasis in

Minimalist Structure stories is on internal conflict. The protagonists are often reactive, rather than proactive. And there can be more than one Hero. These stories are more artistic and ask the Audience to ponder on the questions they raise rather than answer them with a conclusion. They tend to be unsatisfying to most people because they leave you hanging.

SURREAL: Also known as Anti-Structure. This form deals with conflicting realities. It delves into absurdity. Reality has no meaning. There are no rules. Anything goes. And like Minimalist stories, nothing really changes. The characters are pretty much the same going in as they come out. Time is usually broken up and random. Coincidence occurs more often than causality. Examples of this form are: Comics: *Eightball, Sinking*. Movies: *Monty Python and the Holy Grail, Fellini's Roma, Mulholland Drive*

It's possible for a story to fall somewhere between two of these forms. No story has to be purely one form or another.

Classical Structure is the most popular because it's how the Audience sees reality. People want to believe the world is somewhat ordered and things happen for a reason. We all live in linear time and reality seems fairly consistent. Classical structure tries to emulate this. It relates the story in a manner people can believe in. Even though real life is nothing like fiction.

Recently, it's become popular for movies and TV shows, as well as fiction, to play around with classical structure. Linear has become a dirty word in some circles. But linear does not mean the plot should be obvious or predictable. This is a failure in storytelling that trying to trick the audience by telling the story out of order will not necessarily solve.

When choosing to do a story in one of the other two

forms, it's best to start out with a classical structure before you lead your story into the other form. This way, the audience won't be too jarred by what you're about to do.

Take a look at the fiction out there, the movies you have at home, and study their structures. It will tell you a lot about them.

REMEMBER: People prefer stories that emulate reality as they see it.

CONFLICT

All stories arise from conflict. As we stated earlier, the hero wants something. He goes on a quest to obtain the object of desire. What makes it a story is the conflict that stands between the hero and his goal. That is the crux of your story. Conflict keeps stories moving. Lose the conflict and you lose your audience.

Conflict is not action. Many writers mistakenly confuse the two, and thus end up with stories full of meaningless action scenes. Conflict is the *reason* most action occurs. Conflict is when two forces are in opposition to each other. These forces can be emotional, mental, physical, spiritual, sociological, or elemental.

We begin to understand a character through their response to conflict. How each person reacts to any given situation defines their character. We respond to how characters deal with conflict because we can relate to it. Conflict is in our face every single day in one form or another. And when it's not, we're bored.

How a character deals with their conflicts helps us gain perspective on our own lives. It can either serve to validate or repudiate our own choices. If we really disagree with the choices a character makes when dealing with his conflict, we form negative opinions about that character. If we love the choice they make, we love the character more. It's that simple.

So how your characters deal with conflict will have a lot to do with how your audience is going to feel about your work. Remember one crucial thing, however. Conflict is *not* action. They are two completely different things. We'll discuss the nature of action in a later chapter.

Types of Conflict

Conflict comes in several forms. You have to choose the

type that best serves your story. Every form of conflict has implications on the level it affects. They are:

INTERNAL: The conflict a person has with themselves. Inner turmoil. Moral dilemmas. Overcoming trauma. Psychological problems. This conflict is not with other characters, though it can affect other characters in the story. The Internal Conflict is best showcased in the novel, where the Audience feels they are in the mind of the character, because they are visualizing based on the chosen words of the writer. Comics can also handle the internal conflict effectively through use of captions. The art work can show the struggle of the character in many different ways. But the film and theater mediums are much less effective dealing with this form of conflict which is why so many novels don't translate well to film. Novels that deal mainly with external conflicts always translate better than those which deal with internal ones. The internal conflict is about what personal demons or pain stands in the way of them achieving their story goals. Whether they realize it or not. Many people are not honest with themselves about their pain or inner conflicts, and that holds them back. By having a character achieve some sort of break through, an inner conflict is the way for them to move forward and achieve their goal. Failure to do that will result in failure to overcome their obstacle, which may be themselves, or an addiction of some kind.

PERSONAL: This is between the Hero and his friends and lovers. It's about inter-personal relations between individuals. It does not involve larger issues like peer pressure or the rules of society, but rather, the problems people have relating one on one. This is the conflict best showcased in the theater. Though comics handle it well.

EXTERNAL: External conflict is the conflict that's happening to the character, from outside forces. Such as society or culture. The external conflict is concerned with how it stands in the way of our characters goals. Everyone wants something. But we can't have everything we want because something stands in the way. Lack of money, access to something, other people, the law. Your character is faced with this dilemma and dealing with this conflict will be a large part of your story.

ELEMENTAL: Between man and the environment, between the hero and a force of nature. The hero deals with an elemental force which has no persona. It could be anything from a giant meteor heading toward earth or a pack of rabid Chihuahuas.

The Nature of Conflict

By itself, conflict is impersonal. Even it you're dealing with a war. People understand the concept of a war, but they don't see what it has to do with them unless you apply the exercise of conscious will on it, through your main characters. Then it becomes tangible.

If I said two guys were fighting down the street, they'd be faceless individuals in your mind and meaningless to you on a personal level. You don't know who they are or why they're fighting. But if I said your best friend is fighting your worst enemy, all of a sudden the idea draws you in because it now has personal meaning.

That's how you involve the Audience in the conflict. By making the characters people they can identify with as they deal with the conflict. You do this by showing their *dynamic will* in action.

The story of a guy who just wants to have a decent life isn't very exciting. It's a very passive, run-of-the mill desire. There's nothing special about it. Nothing to make the character's struggle interesting.

But...when you show that he will fight the most incredible odds to secure that peaceful life, *then* it becomes interesting, and so does the Hero. You transform the conflict by showing his dynamic will in action against it.

When you're writing a story about personal and/or social conflicts, you are really pitting the will of your characters against each other. And through that use of will, we learn who they are and what they're made of.

In an internal conflict, the character uses their will against their own innate nature. They may have a phobia about fire. To get out of a building they're trapped in, they have to walk through a fire filled room. They must *force* themselves to do something they are afraid to do. They're battling their own desires for a better good.

Lack of internal conflict limits a character's dimension. Single minded individuals are only common in bad fiction. Not in life. Everyone has inner demons of some kind. We're conflicted individuals. According to scientists, reason and emotion are completely intertwined. When someone suffers brain damage to the emotion centers of the brain, they lose the ability to make logical decisions.

This is because we learn by our mistakes. If we no longer fear negative repercussions, we would do anything without thought. So you need to be aware of a characters fears, needs and desires. Their emotional hot buttons.

It will have a big impact on the character's choices.

REMEMBER: All stories arise from conflict. Conflict is transformed by dynamic will.

THE PREMISE

The premise is an important component because it serves as the soul of the story. It's the point. Without it, you have what is known as a "shaggy dog" story, which is a rambling mess without a clue of where it's going.

The premise is the destination your story needs to reach at the end. Try to think of a story as a desert highway stretching out before you. At the end of the road is home (the premise). You want to go home. If you follow the road, you make it. You validate the premise.

But...if you drive off the road and go somewhere else, you're lost. You failed the premise and you're out in the desert without a clue.

A premise is an argument and it's your job to prove it. We'll get into how that's done in a minute, but let's take a look at some examples of a premise.

THE WIZARD OF OZ: "Home is where the heart is." Dorothy ran away from home to save her dog and ended up in a beautiful, sometimes scary place known as Oz where she met a lot of people she came to love as friends. But in the end, she knew that there was no place she'd rather be than home. To her, home was where her loved ones were, even though Oz was much nicer and more interesting than Kansas when you get down to it .

KRAMER VS KRAMER: "Family is more important than a career." Mr. Kramer found himself becoming a father for the first time when his wife left him with his son. Until then, he was too busy to give his kid much attention. Now he had to learn all the things a parent must know, including responsibility for your family. It made him less effective at work, so he lost his job and had to get another. But in the end, his family was the most important thing to him and it also made him more fulfilled as a human being.

MY FAIR LADY: "Men and Women need each other." In this story Henry Higgins is a middle aged bachelor with no time for women. That is, until he decides to teach Eliza Dolittle how to speak and act like an educated lady. Higgins falls in love with her. The story shows that men and women can be independent, but they still need each other to be complete human beings.

GOODFELLAS: "Crime doesn't pay, in the end." The movie tells the life story of real life gangster Henry Hill who worked for the mob since he was a teenager but ended up in witness protection when he got busted and had to rat out his friends.

FORREST GUMP: "Don't give up your dream and you'll eventually be rewarded." Forrest Gump wanted to marry Jenny, and he didn't bother with any other women until she finally came around. He also stuck with the service until they discharged him and did all right. He stuck with the shrimp boat even though he was failing at it and eventually came out rich in the end.

THE DARK KNIGHT: "Heroes become scapegoat if they stick around long enough.' Batman pursues the Joker relentlessly. One of the Joker's counter moves drives DA Harvey Dent insane and he becomes another villain. So much mayhem is committed by all parties that Batman decides to take the blame for Harvey Dent's death and goes into hiding.

So, the premise creates an argument which you have to prove to make the story work. If you fail to make your premise convincing, your story is going to fall flat. If you lack a premise, people will come away from your story feeling they've wasted their time. Premises give a sense of worth to a story. The reason is...

Stories are metaphors for life

Fiction has the power to give meaning to the meaninglessness of life. Life is chaotic and hard to understand for many of us. Fiction can bring order and sense to it all. You, the writer, have the powers of a god when you craft a story. You decide what happens, when, and how. You must construct events in a logical, but unpredictable pattern that points inevitably to the conclusion raised by your premise.

Because stories are about life, understand that *life means change*. Every second of our existence brings us closer to new experiences. It brings us closer to love, sex, money, pain, illness, joy, fear, despair, triumph, and yes...even death. No matter how dull your personal existence may be, change is going to effect your life one way or another. But more importantly, for the Audience, change is something they *need* to see. Anything static is boring. Stories that don't effect the characters or don't make a difference are generally dull stories. There are exceptions to this rule. But we'll explore that later.

Your story needs to effect change on the main characters whether they like it or not. And the changes need to verify the argument of the premise. This is done is by employing the power of *choice.*

The choices your character makes in the course of the story should further enhance the statement of your premise. This way, the Audience lives through the Hero's experiences and witnesses the validation of the premise.

Fact is neutral. Stories are interpretations of facts. You cannot do any documentary without coloring it to your opinion or a theory. You can't tell a story without choosing which "facts" you want to present. Reality is superior to our little paper world. We can only objectify reality through the subjective lens of our minds.

What a good writer does is create *meaning* from all the

events of the story by confirming their premise.

REMEMBER: Until the premise is put to the test of the story's conflicts, it's nothing more than an theory. Your job is to *prove it.*

The Counter Premise

In order to make your premise believable, you have to present compelling arguments for the opposing side. Otherwise, your story becomes preachy and one sided.

This is done via the counter premise.

In most cases, the counter premise is the Villain's agenda. In Kramer Vs Kramer, Mrs. Kramer was trying to get custody of the son. The argument she used in court was that she was a better parent because she now makes more money, she's the mother, and that Mr. Kramer cared more about his job than his family. Her lawyer points out that Kramer lost his job and was now making a lot less, so he isn't a good provider. In other words, "Your career is critical to your family's well being."

This is the counter premise. In the end, the premise wins the argument because the boy chooses his father and the wife sees he has become a better parent because of his choices. His choices validated the story's premise.

Another example, JAWS. In Jaws the premise is: "There are monsters in the ocean. Deal with it!" The counter premise is: "Man doesn't have the right to mess with nature." In order to get the shark, which is the force of nature in the story, they have to go to the shark's element. The sea. It becomes clear that man does not belong out at sea. He is vulnerable, unequipped to survive in the ocean without his precious technology. Indeed, even *with* his technology, nature can win. The hero of the story barely survives, only with cunning. His choice is to adapt as best he can. And by making this choice, rather than giving in, he validates the premise.

The counter premise needs to be a compelling argument. Perhaps as compelling or almost more so than the premise. When the counter premise is used properly, the Audience worries about the hero. Your hero is the champion of the premise, whether he's aware of it or not.

Finding your Premise

When you begin to formulate your story, you may not know what the premise is. That's okay. You can find out what it is when you have more of the plot constructed. The premise isn't something you need to have in mind from the beginning. Even if you have it in mind, you may find it changes as the story unfolds. Stories by nature are organic. As characters come alive, as scenes take shape, new meanings and insights can form. This can alter your original premise. So first, figure out who your characters are, what they want, what the Grail is, then start putting scenes together. Soon after, you'll start to see a pattern take shape. The Premise will come into clarity. Then you can fine tune the story until your premise and counter premise battle it out with the kind of effectiveness your story needs.

Whatever you do, never tell the audience point blank what your premise is. If you need to have a character say it out loud, you're showing how ineffective you are as a writer. The audience should be able to get the point on their own. Once you start preaching, you start boring.

Once you've found your premise, evaluate the scenes you've come up with and see if they can't be modified to make the arguments that you need to make. In the Star Trek film GENERATIONS, the premise is explored in almost every scene. The film's premise is:

"Life is short, so make your mark the best way you can." Picard is always regretting the fact that he never had a family. This is echoed by Kirk, as well. To these men, a family is how they would have liked to made their mark. But by the end of the story both men realize their destiny is to save the world and bringing justice and peace to the galaxy. They recognize they've mattered in the scheme of things and find their peace in that.

If you study this film, you'll notice the writers squeezed the premise into almost every scene. It gives the story more resonance.

You can also use subplots to play off the premise with themes. A subject we will delve into at length in a later chapter. Just remember that a story without a premise is a story without a soul.

REMEMBER: The story must show conflict between the Premise and the Counter Premise. A strong Counter Premise makes for a strong story.

METAPHORS

The dictionary defines this as a figure of speech in which a word or phrase is applied to an object or action to which it is not literally applicable. For example: "I'm weeping a pool of tears." But in a story context metaphors can be a theme that you use in a story to give it substance.

The English word "metaphor" originates from the Greek metaphorá, which means "to transfer" or "to carry over." A metaphor transfers meaning from one subject on to another so that the target subject can be understood in a new way. By defining something metaphorically, you create a powerful symbol that can be used in your story.

Here is how a metaphor can be used in a larger sense. In JRR Tolkien's *The Hobbit*, Smaug the Dragon is one of the villains of the story. But the story has a larger theme about insatiable greed. The dwarves in the story are a race in love with gems and gold from under the earth. They want their mountain full of treasure back which was stolen in the past by Smaug. But what is a dragon but a metaphor for greed. Dragons covert gold and kill for it, but it is something they have no use for since they don't eat it and can't spend it. All they do is hoard it. Which is basically what the dwarves did with it and intend to do with it. Once the dwarves get their hands on it again they have no plans to share it with anyone, even though many people who helped them lost their cities and lives in the process. The gold also inspires greed from the goblins who want to take it from the dwarves. In the middle of this is the main character, Bilbo Baggins, who doesn't care about wealth and serves as a conscience for the other characters.

Greed is played out in various way as metaphors in this novel (and film) to great effect. This is something you can do in your story. Pick something you want to discuss and use metaphors so that you aren't beating people over the head with it. They are a very handy and often powerful way to get an idea across without being obvious to your intention.

One of the greatest sins a writer can commit is to preach a message. No one likes being preached to except the converted. Your job is to convince people that your message is correct. As we will discuss later, your story will be about something. Metaphors are a tool you can use to symbolize a thing, an experience, a place, a person, a monster, etc. Using them drives home a point you want to make indirectly.

It's important to remember that a lot of things in life can serve as perfect metaphors. As an exercise, start thinking of possible metaphors you can use in dialog, or as thematic symbols. It will make your job more fun.

Allegory

You can make a whole story that's a metaphor. It's called an allegory. An allegory is a complete story with an extended metaphor throughout to illustrate complex ideas in a comprehensible way. Many writers have used genres like historical or science fiction to tell an allegorical story. The movie *High Noon* was an allegory about McCarthyism and the hero was metaphorically standing up against the injustice the outlaws were bringing to town. Here is a good example how you can tell a story using metaphors without preaching because the movie is a classic and McCarthyism is a historical footnote. The film lives on because it's metaphor is universal and thus can be seen in different ways by future generations. You don't want to date your work by being too literal. Metaphors and allegories can work to your advantage.

Setting a story in the past or a future society removes it

from the politics of the now. You can say what you want to say without beating people over the head with a message about something that may be forgotten a few years after your story comes out. The best fiction deals with universal truths. Those kind of stories stand the test of time.

Issues and problems aren't that diverse in reality. They always call into similar camps. The players change but song remains the same. So by changing the time and place, you can talk about issues near and dear to your heart without turning into a lecturer. The story's demands will require you to think it out clearly and who knows, you might learn a thing or two in the process.

REMEMBER: Remove your story from the present to make the plot more universal.

THE MILIEU

The Milieu is the world of your story. More specifically, it's the reality in which the story takes place. If your story was set in a Seattle high school in 1942, that's a different world than a Detroit High School in 1996. If you set your story on the island of Manhattan in 1600, that's a different world than Manhattan today.

Your Milieu must be a place Audiences can believe in. It can be as fantastic as you want it to be, but it must obey certain rules, contain certain truths, or it will be a mess no one will want to revisit. In tourism terms, it can be as enjoyable as Maui or as unpleasant as Newark. It's all up to you.

Your Milieu becomes attractive to the Audience when you make it believable. You can set your story in Hell, and it can still real to us as long as it's fully drawn, and I don't mean by the artist. Because when we feel a story world is a half-baked mess, we tend to get distracted. The Milieu must live!

Your Milieu also establishes the limitations imposed on the characters. Limitations are good things to know because they are tools for adding pressure and making the heroes lives more difficult. People respond to limitations, because most of us have to live with them every day.

To make your world live and breath it's a good idea to answer some, or all, of the following questions.

1. Time and place: Is it on a cruise ship in the Caribbean? Does it take place in a ghetto on the planet Zander? Is it happening among the social gatherings of the of the French Bourgeoisie in 1887 or does it happen in a Gay Disco in 1978? The place should be clear in your mind so you have a point of reference to draw from, and so the Audience will have a feel for the milieu. If you choose a place you are unfamiliar with, like say...Addis Ababa, make sure you do your research so you can write about it with authority. Otherwise, it will seem generic and unreal to the Audience. If you're creating your own world, make a list of all the things unique and interesting about the place and try to incorporate them into your story. This will give the milieu the life it needs to make it believable.

One of the reasons J.R.R. Tolkien's Middle Earth remains so popular is because he spent an incredible amount of time making sure he knew his Milieu inside and out. He wrote volumes of notes, compiled the histories of families and places, created languages and alphabets. Middle Earth really feels like a real place to many people. So does the Vampire society of Anne Rice's novels. She thought everything through and researched her history and locations well. The X Files TV series draws a lot of people into its paranoid, spooky Milieu by following the other rules of the world. Every X-Files story takes place somewhere in the US, a real city, and in present time. But the world of the story is a Milieu where UFOs, Monsters, and government agents are all part of some big conspiracy. The creators of that show spent a lot of time working out the rules of that Milieu. This is why it was so compelling to its fans.

How many stories have you experienced which took place in some generic locale and you felt no connection to it? Making a believable Milieu goes a long way to making the story enjoyable. If you don't connect to the Milieu, you don't connect to the story.

2. Economics: What kind of financial realities do the characters have to deal with? Are they rich like Bruce Wayne, or poor like Spiderman? Are goods available for money, or is there rationing? What is the economic system the Milieu employs? Remember that economics affect your characters just like they affect you and me. If there's anything that smacks of unreality, it's characters who have no apparent job, yet always have money for every situation. People respond better to what they can relate to. In most people's case, cash flow is limited.

3. Politics: Naturally, the politics of your Milieu can have a major impact on the story. If you set it in a society under a tyrannical ruler or government, such as the Milieu we saw in *1984*, *Brazil*, or *Schindler's List*, its going to have an impact on your characters. Just as economics play a part in shaping how your characters survive in your Milieu, so does the politics. If the politics are modern day America, you still need to examine whether this will effect your Hero. If your Hero is an illegal alien in South Texas, the politics of the Milieu are possibly going to effect him.

4. Power: This is somewhat related to the previous question but not necessarily. In the world of your story, certain people may have power over your character's lives, but not necessarily politically. They could be doctor treating your hero, they could be the banker who decides whether they get that loan, they could be the hero's boss. The power structure of your Milieu is important to the character's life, especially if it is part of the plot in any. So examine how it affects them and the story.

5. Morals, Ethics, and Laws: What are the unique morals, ethics, and laws in your milieu? If your story is set in the Disco era of the late 70s, failure to pass around a joint could be construed as bad morals, whereas in the late 80s, smoking a joint would be considered bad morals. Ethics? In a strict Muslim Family it's not unethical to kill a daughter who is promiscuous. Nor is it unlawful or immoral. But it is in the Western Milieu. So, you can have a conflict of Milieus within your story. There have been cases in the U.S. where this has happened and the parents were arrested. In the Milieu of their family, this was not wrong, but it was in the Milieu of the society they chose to live in. Morals, Ethics and Laws will have an impact on your character in some way because it will either determine their choices, or effect the consequences of their actions. You can't really ignore them or people won't believe in your Milieu.

6. Values: What are the moral values in your Milieu? By what standards do people live, or are there any? Values gives the story and characters some grounding. That's important for realism's sake.

7. Rituals: How do people go about certain tasks in your Milieu? When people meet, here in the west, they usually shake hands. In Japan, they bow to each other. These are rituals, but there are so many others. Giving a woman flowers on a date is a ritual. So is having turkey on Thanksgiving. In your Milieu there will be rituals of some kind and they can be used to establish the uniqueness of your world, as well as define the way characters interact. You can also use them to symbolize elements of your story.

8. Backstory: When you're dealing with other Milieus, dimensions, or history, it's a good idea to know what the story behind these things are (the backstory). It may be necessary to put the backstory in your plot somewhere, in a non-obtrusive way so your Audience can understand the history that shaped your world. It will usually have an effect on the story, regardless. If you wrote the tale of a black man in Mississippi circa 1952, the backstory of that place would have an effect on your plot. No doubt about it.

Research your Milieu

I cannot stress the importance of this more. Research is critical. If you're writing about something you made up, like an alien world, it's still a good idea to research how similar cultures, economies, religions work as a model for what you create. Depth is everything.

Besides, research provides you with ideas and insights that will help your creative process as you build your story. A lot of good characters, plot twists, and scenes can come from real life examples you can find by doing research. And research is one of the best the best cures for clichés there is. Clichés come from ignorance. Research is education.

If you were to write a story about a cop working in the Mission District of San Francisco, talking to cops in that district and hearing their stories would give you tons of material and ideas, in addition to getting the facts straight. Then you'd have a fresh story instead of something inspired by half-baked memories of bad TV shows.

Ideas write themselves when you know your Milieu. Research not only deters clichés, it's also a good cure for writer's block. Reading expands the mind, provides fresh insights. And talking to people with useful experience can give you a zillion story possibilities.

Your Milieu will live when it has depth. Depth comes from knowledge and experience. If you're not an expert on the Milieu you're writing, make sure you are before you get too far into it. Your Audience will thank you for it.

And finally, the rules of your Milieu need to be internally consistent. Internal consistency means authenticity. Don't establish rules then break them for no reason. You'll destroy the credibility of your Milieu and all that work will be for nothing.

REMEMBER: Believable Milieus make for interesting stories.

TIME

This naturally affects your story as much as the Milieu does. A story takes place in a pocket of time. It can be anything from a second to a thousand years. You need to decide how much time there is.

Once you make that decision, it should effect your story. Because it gives you parameters in which to work. Parameters are a good thing, because it helps you decide how much time your hero has to perform his quest. It also makes the story seem more real. We all live in time. We relate to time limits. We do not relate to endless time. Or time having no meaning. In this modern world especially, time is very important.

The Ticking Clock

Now that you have an idea what the time frame is, it's a good idea to introduce the Ticking Clock. The ticking clock is a literary device which adds urgency to your story. It sets a time limit under which the hero must perform a task. If he fails to achieve his goal by the time limit, he loses. Either his life, the world's life, the love of his life, whatever.

You can employ one or more ticking clocks to a story. Each sub plot can have a ticking clock, but you don't want to burden a story with too many.

A classic example of the ticking clock is the bomb set to go off by a certain time and the hero has to find it. But the T.C. can be as simple as the time a student has to finish his exam, or as complex as the time it takes to woo someone before the risk of taking too long to get to the seduction bores them.

The main purpose of the ticking clock is to add pressure on your character. Pressure is the key to making a story exciting. We'll delve into this subject later.

Night and Day

There are environmental considerations to the time frame, as well. If your story takes place at night, you have to consider the limitations that imposes. Lack of light in certain places can work for or against your hero. The fact that most people are sleeping means less bystanders or witnesses around. But it also means people are home and might call the police when they hear a commotion going on outside. There are other considerations to night. A married person should normally be with their spouse at night. What if they aren't? This could be telling.

Day time imposes other considerations. Sunlight can be good or bad, depending whether or not you're a vampire. It can mean hot weather, it can mean more people are out on the street. More witnesses to the action. More bystanders who can get killed. This can impact on your story. You have to be aware of the effect daytime has on your plot. It adds to the realism.

Personally, I like to set a lot of my action scenes at night so there will be less bystanders around. It gives you less to worry about. It also lets you play with mood, lighting, and contrasts. But sometimes bystanders are nice to have around.

Weather

Technically, this is an environmental subject, but I'm including it under the Time Frame because weather can hinder your hero as he races against the ticking clock. A blizzard can make it real hard to get from here to there. Same goes for a hurricane, or fog, or a rain storm.

Weather also adds a sense of atmosphere to your story and can make it seem more real. Too many comic books have perfect weather all the time. It makes things a little too convenient. As we'll explain later, you want to put pressure on your characters. You want to make it really hard for them to reach their goal. Otherwise, the story is boring. Weather is a good way to put pressure on your characters. Especially since it's a hard thing to change.

REMEMBER: Time is valuable! Night and Day have implications. Weather creates limitations.

THE OBJECT OF DESIRE

The Hero and the Villain have conflicting motives when it comes to the focus of the story known as "The Object of Desire". It is often called the MacGuffin. I prefer to use the term "Grail".

The Grail is whatever the hero thinks will restore balance to his life. There may be a visible grail in the story. A material object. But the Grail can be something intangible like friendship or trust.

All stories are about A>B<C. The Hero (A) wants C (the Grail) and B (the Villain/Conflict) stands in the way. In almost every case, the Grail can be summed up as that which restores balance, because stories always begin with the hero's life being upset by some event. The hero then sets out to restore balance to his life. The grail is his means of achieving that balance.

In the case of E.T., the Grail was E.T. being able to return to his people unmolested. The Villain's goal was to capture and study him. So freedom is the Grail, and the Villains are in direct opposition to it.

Action, Crime, and Suspense stories usually employ a physical Grail. Examples are a piece of microfilm, a suitcase full of cash, a nuclear bomb, plans to a new secret weapon, or incriminating documents. Writers call this kind of grail "MacGuffins". Sometimes the Hero is already in possession of the MacGuffin, but doesn't know how to use it. So the Grail in such stories is knowledge. Knowledge restores the balance.

Romance stories have an obvious Grail, love. The Villain is either a rival lover, parents, society, or nature, threatening to keep the lovers apart.

Sometimes the Grail is a person or a living creature. The Grail in Jaws was the shark, doubling as Villain and

Grail. In cop movies the Grail is the capture or death of the criminal (Villain). In some stories, the object is the rescue or capture of a person who only serves as the Grail and not as an Villain. Charles Bronson did a movie called *Breakout*, where the Grail was a man in a Mexican prison that Bronson was supposed to "break out". In *Stark Trek: Into Darkness*, the villain Khan is the grail. First he's the villain, then an ally, only to end up the villain again. He still is the focus of the heroes.

Most writers view Grails as physical objects of desire. But since all stories are about someone trying to get something, or not get something as the case may be (refusal is an action), we can define any object of desire as a Grail. It doesn't have to be a material thing.

When you sit down to create a story and are stuck for where to begin, it's not a bad idea to think about what the Grail might be. That makes it easier to then formulate the motivations of the Villain and the Hero. Once you have those things figured out, everything starts falling into place.

Unconscious Desire

A hero has a conscious desire in a story to win the Grail. But you can also establish an unconscious desire on the hero's part. A desire he may not be aware of, but his actions betray. This desire is often radically different than his conscious one.

When unconscious desire is employed, it can add a lot of dimension to the work. The object of the unconscious desire becomes the true grail in the story and all the hero's conscious desires are ephemeral.

The true grail in these scenarios becomes the "Super objective". No other MacGuffin or Grail really matters when you're dealing with an unconscious desire, because the U.D. is what the story is about.

When you're dealing with a super objective, the conscious desire is a front. A ruse, even. Sometimes the false grail is to establish that the Hero has sold out his personal values for what he perceives to be a higher purpose. But the story teaches him that his "heart's desire" is more important than what he's been fighting for. During the Crisis, he realizes what his heart's desire truly is after a series of events makes it clear to him, and this is when he makes his choice.

This desire is usually at odds with the interests of other protagonists in the story, but as far as the premise is concerned, choosing to follow it is the right thing for him to do in this story.

REMEMBER: The unconscious desire is the only desire that matters when it's used.

BACKSTORY

I use this term quite a bit in the course of this book and now I'll delve into what it means. Basically this refers to the history of your character or story setting. It's what you need to know when you write something, so you and the Audience are not left in the dark trying to figure things out. It's a set of events invented for a plot, presented as preceding and leading up to that plot.

Backstory was first described by Aristotle as the moment when a character makes a critical discovery. This moment of realization informs the Audience of some kind of history that took place beforehand. But a backstory is also something that you formulate beforehand when you are putting your story together. It's the secret history that you will want to unfold in the course of your tale. It's always good to know where a character is from, what they experienced, where they are going, what they want. What kind of upbringing did they have. Are they religious? Are they political? Are they talented? This is all backstory material that will play a part either in your current story or a sequel.

Know your characters. Know your settings. Know your world.

Work out your character's backstory. Work out your setting if it's required. Work out the milieu if needed. The better your back story, the more believable your story will be.

As I mention elsewhere, three great writers for backstory are George R.R.Martin, author of *Game of Thrones* and many others. J.R.R. Tolkien, author of *the Hobbit* and *Lord of the Rings* and Stephen King, author of a zillion other books like *The Stand, It, The Shining, Under The Dome*. All of these writers invest a serious amount of time into backstory. Tolkien spent 30 years on The Lord of the Rings backstory. More, in fact since he began his *Silmarillion* when he was in WWI. The book wasn't published until 1976. Steven King's *It* is a marvel for the history he tells of the fictional town of Derry, Maine. George R.R. Martin's *A Song of Ice and Fire* books have a wealth of backstory for every family and nation in his world. These are great writers to study, and there are many more. They can show you how it's done.

Writers like Edgar Rice Burroughs, who gave us Tarzan and John Carter of Mars did it in the pages of pulp magazines. You can do it sparingly if you must, but people like to learn about the fictional worlds they are reading, even if it's in a historical novel.

If you want characters to be believed, you also need to make their story convincing. Your story has a story and so does your characters. Their story fleshes out your over all story. You can make it as normal or crazy as you want but it has to be believable. Making it believable is done, in part, by having things in a character's past effect the story. A character may have buried feelings because of something in their past. This causes them to act out in your story. Having it revealed as a backstory event helps give that scene agency.

REMEMBER: Every story needs backstories.

BELIEVABILITY

Truth is subjective, not objective. We all don't recognize the same truths.

All men are created equal? There's a lot of people who disagree on that one.

God is love? Tell that to someone with cancer.

The earth is round? Scientists say it's oval. Some people still think it's flat.

In fiction, the writer's job is to establish truth. We have to show what truth is for the world of our story. Convince your Audience and you'll not only validate the premise, you may even make them feel good. Fail, and you're going to be laughed at, your story tossed in the trash heap of history.

So, if truth is subjective...meaning we all see it differently, then how do we establish it in the story? Well, this book tells you various means to achieve that. But since the goal of this book is to make story structure simple to understand I will boil it down to a few simple maxims as an appetizer for the main course.

We all understand certain things from our own experiences. We may disagree on most of them, but we all agree on one thing.

Life doesn't happen exactly the way we want it to. Even billionaires have bad days.

This is why conflict is so important to making a story work. Conflict stands between us and our goal. We relate to it. We understand it. *And we want to beat it!*

Truth is established by showing the best way to overcome that conflict. We do that by systematically testing and rejecting every action until we arrive at the premise. Every scene serves that purpose. No scene should be empty of purpose. Scenes test the premise in one way or another. When all the tests are completed, we arrive at our conclusion.

But the tests have to be valid. They have to be something we can believe in. They can't be illogical or nonsensical. And more importantly, they must have emotional resonance for us. Logic and emotion must be married in a story for it to develop the kind of power it needs. When logic is married with emotional resonance, we create meaning.

Stories create change for the characters through conflict. Because truth is subjective, we arrive at truth when it has meaning for us. So make sure your story creates meaningful truth.

SUSPENSION OF DISBELIEF

All writers are liars.

No story is true, even if it's based in fact. Things inevitably get left out. All stories are one sided, even when they try not to be.They are written from the perspective of the writer. Someone always wins. Someone always loses.

So, you've got to convince your Audience that these fables you're spinning are the gospel truth. Obviously, they will know better. But they want to believe. People desire entertainment. Our minds seek to escape for awhile. So you have an opening.

The balance of the Audience's willingness to be sucked in and your ability to keep them off guard is where technique and structure come in. As we discussed earlier, people expect reality to come at them a certain way. Classic story structure imitates life as people see it. But the flow of the action isn't enough. The action has to be believable to them.

To do this you need to create plausible, empathetic characters. You have to create a Milieu they can believe in and enjoy. And you have you present information in an unobtrusive, interesting manner. If you fail to do any of these things, you are going to find yourself with a bored or disenchanted audience.

When the Audience is on your side, they're your friend. They'll love you. They'll praise you to the high heavens. But when they don't like your work, they're your enemy. They will bad mouth you and your stories to anyone who will listen. So it's extremely important that you try to win them over. Their good will has a lot to do with how successful your career is going to be.

Your job is to seduce them. You want them to get in bed with you and stay there until you're finished. So remember the three rules of story seduction:

1. Create believable, empathetic characters.

2. Create a fascinating, credible Milieu.

3. Tell them what they need to know. No cheap surprises.

4. Respect the Audience. Don't treat them like idiots.

REMEMBER: Respect the audience like you would like to be respected.

Story Structure

"Easy reading is damn hard writing."
Nathaniel Hawthorne

ACT STRUCTURE

We've been discussing various elements of story construction such as the world, the plot, the premise and the characters. Now we get down to the nitty gritty.

Act Structure is the most classic form of story construction. It's a system that has worked incredibly well for thousands of years. I'm going to give you the basics so you can apply these principals you see fit.

Most of us are familiar with the structure known as the three act play. In a nutshell, the three act structure is: The Beginning, the Middle, and the End of the story.

In comic books, this structure has become rarer as writers tend to leave their audiences hanging with unresolved climaxes at the end of every issue. Most comics are serialized fiction after all. But there is a right way and a wrong way to handle cliffhangers.

For now let's deal with the acts.

What is an Act?

Acts are blocks of scenes in a story, separated by act climaxes ("Turning Points"). A comics story is built up from this form: Panel>Scene>Sequence>Acts>Story. Every other medium employs the same form except for the panels. Panels are unique to comics.

The act serves to show a major change taking place in the story. It's composed of sequences which build to that change, which is the turning point. The sequences are composed of scenes and the scenes are made up of the individual story panels.

The act serves to create a sense of closure for one part of the story. The audience can't take everything at the same level of energy. We control the energy of the story through these compartmental devices. An act is the sum total of all its parts and it propels us into the next act until the climax and resolution.

Despite what many people think, the three act structure is not the most effective way to tell a story. Shakespeare preferred to do his plays in five acts. A story can be told in one act or seven depending on the objectives of the plot. Acts build the story's emotional charge. If it takes more than three acts to build up the proper charge, then so be it.

Let's focus on one and two act stories for a second. These kinds of stories are by nature, brief. The longer the story, the more complexity and reversals are needed, and thus more acts.

One Act

One act stories are usually very short. They have the "twist" or "surprise" ending. These stories are created in service of the ending. Everything leads up to a big surprise. The old E.C. Comics stories were written using this principle. Bill Gaines would come up with some twist ending idea and bounce it off his collaborator Al Feldstien. They would often write the story backwards from the ending. This is not a bad idea, actually, and it worked well for them. The ending is one of the most important components of a story. But we'll deal with that later. One act stories are pretty much reserved for short fiction because you don't want to take too long getting to the punchline. The comic gag strip, such as "Garfield", use the one act story structure. The structure of a three panel strip is: Setup, Beat, Punchline. The beat being a pause of some kind before you hit them with the joke.

Two Act

Two Act stories are often used in half hour TV sitcoms. The first act takes place before the commercial break in the middle. Its purpose is to get the characters into trouble. The second act gets them out again. Hopefully, the climax of the second act will have a slam bang ending with a nice twist. This format isn't bad for one issue comic book stories. Especially if they're simple action plots. But the three act structure is probably best.

Three Act

This is the most widely used structure, mainly because it's the most simple for a long form story like a movie. It's also the minimum number of acts needed to take the hero through all four of the story values. One and two act stories are mainly gimmick stories aimed at reaching a simple conclusion rather than exploring the depths of a character or their experience. With the three act structure, we can really begin to get down and dirty.

Three Acts Broken Down

Act one serves to introduce the main characters, define their motivations, show us the Trigger Event, and get the story in motion for the second act. It's basically an introduction to the story. But it needs to grab our attention and not let us go. It's usually not that big a section of the over all story. And it ends with a plot twist that turns the story in the direction of the conflict.

Act two is the section where progressive complications threaten to defeat the hero. The villain/conflict gains his ascendancy in this act and is winning by the end of it. This is largest act in terms of size. It's where most of the action takes place, where most of the character development occurs. You need to pace this section well and build it carefully for the big twist that throws us headlong into the climax.

Act three is the climax and resolution of the story. It is the smallest act in size and for good reason. Like its namesake, the climax doesn't take long, but boy is it powerful! We couldn't take too much of the climax at once. It would destroy it's power. Energy in a story is a critical thing to control and the climax is an explosion of all the pent up energy we've been building. It's where the forces of the conflict are at their peak. It's here where the winner is determined and the outcome is revealed. The resolution is going to have to be short, because a long resolution makes for a dragged out ending. I'm sure you've seen them before and know what they feel like. So the third act is where we finish the story with our final body blow to the audience, and then we wrap it up nice and sweet so they don't lose that warm, glowing feeling the climax gave them.

Constructing the Acts

Now that we have a rough idea what acts are and what purpose they serve, let's talk about how we put them together.

Every act is composed of sequences. Sequences exist to create the Turning Point/Act Climax. They tell the story of how the Turning Point/Act Climax came about. Every sequence builds energy to create a lesser turning point which throws us into the following sequence. The last sequence in an act ends with a major turning point.

Sequences are composed of scenes. Scenes are events that, when placed together, form the story of the sequence. Scenes end with mini-turning points that are smaller that the ones that end a sequence. Except for the last scene in the last sequence. These turning points can be as subtle as a change of expression on a person's face, or as powerful as a planet exploding. It all depends on where they are in the sequence.

In comics, panels are used to create the scenes. It's possible to do a scene in one panel, but generally, a scene is made up of two or more panels. Each panel is a static image showing a snapshot of action taking place. There will be dialog, narration, and possibly sound effects to make this static image come alive in some way. But these devices are not always needed. Panels are the only element of the act structure that does not end with a turning point. Not unless they are the last panel in a scene.

So...how do we construct an act? We start from the first image in panel one. Many people like to start with the "Splash Page", a single panel page that has a dynamic image to rouse our interest. This first image sets the mood for the story right off the bat.

You can set the mood of the story with the first scene and take it from there. Once you establish the mood, you have to work within its confines. Changing the mood of story once it's been set can be a difficult and dangerous thing to do. I'm sure you've read books or seen films where it was unclear whether it was a comedy or a drama. This is because they set one mood, then changed it, then changed it again.

It's important to either keep the mood consistent, or build toward a change in mood at the act climax. Don't try to make a major mood change mid act or you will make it difficult for the audience to decide how to feel about the story.

In prose or a screenplay you would tell the scene by establishing the location and the characters. You start off with a certain energy either positive or negative, like things start off well, then the scene ends with a downturn (or up turn depending on your goal). No scene should end with the same polarity as it started. Let me explain.

Story Energy

Before we go further it's important to understand the concept of polarity. Every action has a polarity in story terms. Positive or negative. Non action is neutral. But as we discussed before, neutral does nothing, so it must be used sparingly.

When I say action, I mean that which is done in the scene. So if it's just two people having a conversation, the action could be a positive mood, such as the telling of a joke, or a negative mood maker like your character saying they have a terminal illness.

We either start a scene with a positive or negative. Positive means things are going well for someone (pleasure), negative means things are going bad (pain). If it isn't clear what's happening then it's neutral until we know better.

Every scene starts either positive or negative. And whatever the polarity of the beginning, the end should have reverse polarity. Otherwise the scene exhibited no change. Nothing happened. Everything evened out.

It's possible to switch from neutral to negative or positive. In the case of an opening scene, maybe we started with an establishing shot of a house. There's nothing positive or negative about a shot like that unless you show a missile coming down on the house, or show a party going on in the front yard with people having a good time. Failing that, the shot is neutral. Starting neutral means an undynamic opening. It's your choice.

Polarity allows you to build the story energy, leading up to the Turning Point. Just as every scene starts with a certain polarity and ends with the opposite polarity, so should the sequence and so should the act. This gives the audience a feeling that things are happening. Tensions are building.

When you start positive and end negative, that shows change in the status quo, from good to bad. Reverse the polarity at the beginning and ending of a scene and you have a scene change from bad to good. You can go from negative to negative or positive to positive, but it should be a huge jump in polarity intensity so we feel something happened.

The level of intensity is determined by how strong the charge is. A weak negative charge is a customer saying "No thanks" to a waiter offering dessert. A strong negative charge would be him shooting the waiter between the eyes. A weak positive charge would be the customer saying "Okay, what's your pies today?" A strong positive would be the customer giving the waiter a million dollar tip. .

Audiences need to feel an ebb and flow. A steady stream of positive or negative is wearing. Too much positive is boring. Too much negative is a downer. Too much neutral puts you to sleep. You need to alternate the polarities of your scenes, as well as the strength of the charge. So you might start with mild charges and slowly build toward your climax. Or you might start medium and then lower the charges from there and then build them up again as you go along. You should have lower charged scenes every now and then between high voltage scenes to keep the energy from being too wearing on the reader. Some people call these "quiet moments", and they serve a good purpose when used properly.

It's also important to note that the next scene, sequence, or act, should begin with a different polarity than the previous one ended. If you go from negative to negative, the audience starts feeling depressed. If you go from positive to positive it's not interesting. Too many negatives or positives in a row and the energy level starts to drop in the audience's mind. The charges should go the way *you* want them to go. It's okay to link charges if we're building toward an act climax. Then you can go from bad to worse, from good to great, spending on your goal. But save that kind energy flow for last.

Neutral charges can be like throwing a bucket of cold

water on someone. It can take all the fun out of things. So beware of neutral charges. Use them only when you want to deal with irony or are starting a story. They can be used to bridge scenes with extreme polarities, if you want to create quiet moments, but again, think carefully when using them.

Because we're dealing with a visual medium, we have a lot of choice in how we present data to the audience's eye. Text can add the charge, but one has to be careful using copy without a supporting image. Copy requires you to take the time to read it. An image can tell you something instantly. If you're relying on copy, make sure it's short and sweet.

REMEMBER: Start positive, end negative, or visa-versa

ACT STRUCTURE IN SERIALIZED FICTION

This mainly concerns comics but can also apply to serialized prose stories.

This is a very difficult thing to pull off well, but it's also extremely important to understand if you have to do it.

Just as each story needs to build toward a climax, so does each act. And a serialized comic story in multiple parts can be viewed from this same perspective. Each issue should have a structure, building toward a crisis or climax. At the end of the story is a turning point which throws the momentum of that issue toward the next. This should be done in a compelling enough manner to make us want to read the next one. Make us want it BAD!

The concept of story polarity becomes extremely useful when we deal with serialized fiction. We need to start positive, end negative or visa versa, and with a vengeance! The end of each story must make us really want more. To do that you have to show a build in story energy toward that climax.

The ebb and flow between the Hero and the Villain should become more and more frenzied in each issue. The first issue's tensions build toward a climax that's level 2 in strength. The next issue needs to build to level 3. The following issue needs to build even higher until it can't go any further. Then, that's when you end it.

But the audience doesn't want story arcs longer than five or six issues anymore. It's really hard to sustain their interest that long. Even then, you're pushing it. Long, drawn out epics will earn you a plethora of ill will if you aren't careful. And then it's hard to woo the readers back to the book.

Keep those story arcs short and sweet. Three issues is plenty in most cases. It's hard to sustain story energy over too many acts. You start to experience diminishing returns. The audience has a hard time remembering plot details from month to month. You can't expect them to do that. Especially if they read a lot of titles.

Your set ups shouldn't be paid off three issues later. People are confused easily these days. The Audience has developed a taste for instant gratification, so you have to get to the point. Therefore, it's advisable to make your stories tight. Get those points across quickly and succinctly and build toward a story climax soon.

Single issue stories tend to be a lot more satisfying for the readers. They get a complete package for the price of their comic. They get a fix on who each character is and what they're about. When you come into the middle of some multi-part epic, it tends to be confusing.

With the price of comics being what they are these days, it's suicide to expect people to fork out the money for a multi-part story unless it's one of the coolest things they've read in a long while. Single issue stories are more satisfying. They tend to be what sells a new reader on a book. Alan Moore established himself well on SWAMP THING with "Anatomy Lessons" and other one issue tales. Grant Morrison sold new readers on ANIMAL MAN with one issue stories like "Coyote Gospel" and "Death of the Red Mask". Neil Gaiman probably sold more readers with his one issue stories in SANDMAN because, again, they are complete reads for the price of a single comic. Nothing shows the merit of a writer's talent better than a single issue story. To date, my most financially successful comics were LEX LUTHOR: THE UNAUTHORIZED BIOGRAPHY and HARDCASE #1...both single issue stories.

Also, when you have to pay more money to read the rest of a story it seems like a rip off. Especially when the story wasn't that great to begin with.

The Audience wants a pay off. They want consequences in their stories, not just fight scenes they've seen a million times already. They aren't shelling out four bucks or more for nothing. If nothing is what they get, nothing is what your readership is going to be. Sooner than you think.

It's a rare story that can sustain readership over a long haul. WATCHMEN did it, but it was also a limited series. The readers knew they would only have to buy 12 issues to get the whole story. And it kept most of them interested enough to keep reading.

The two or three issue arc is the safest bet for most continued stories. If you really need more than three issues, you'd better make it worth the while of the Audience. There must be truly original surprises and pay offs in each issue. There must be a sense of great momentum. Failure to achieve that will result in huge drop offs in readership.

When you continue a story, make sure the turning point at the end is a major surprise. The villain standing over the apparently dead or unconscious form of the hero is *not* a surprising ending. It's an ending that has been flogged to death since the 1970s. Nowadays, you need a turning point that has major implications for the character. It raises an urgent question in the mind of the reader: "Oh, god! How the hell are they going to straighten THIS out!?"

The old, Villain standing over the unconscious Hero scene does not raise that question. Because everyone thinks: "Oh, he's just going to wake up, the villain is going to spill his plans, and then the hero will beat him." They've seen it a zillion times already. Even if you plan a different scene in the next issue, it doesn't matter. The audience has already decided what will happen and thirty days later they may not be interested in buying your story to continue.

You must give them a *real* reason to come back. It must be so compelling they are quaking like junkies experiencing withdrawal until that next issue comes out. This can be done with a major reversal using story values, a subject we delve into shortly.

And if you can't pull off a great cliffhanger, write a one issue story, dammit!

REMEMBER: Keep those story arcs short and sweet. One issue stories are best.

PANELS

This page refers to comics panels. So if you aren't writing comics, you can skip ahead to scenes.

Every picture isn't worth a thousand words. I can describe a panel in five. But regardless, these are extremely important components of your story. They are the beats in a scene.

Comics are like visual songs. The text is the lyrics. The art is the music. You need to think of it that way when you write. Each panel is going to make the scene go up or down. They are the notes that you hear in the visual song.

Think about the images you choose to present. These images have to have weight and power. They have to be interesting and informative. And they have to provide some kind of insight to the characters. If someone is merely talking, choose their facial expressions and body language carefully. Make sure you aren't wasting time with boring shots.

Of course, if you're only writing the script, you're dependent on the artist and he may choose to ignore your descriptions, but you can't worry about that. Do what you think is right. You can always argue with the artist later if they draw something different.

Your job is to create feeling with every shot. Emotion is short. It only serves to make feeling specific. An audience cannot sustain emotions for long while reading a story. Mood is no substitute for emotion so don't hold back those gut punches when you need them. Save those intense panels for your turning points and climaxes.

There will be times you introduce a location or a character. In those shots make sure we get a good look at all the relevant things we need to see. Establish them well. Clarity is the most important thing. The less there is in a panel to distract us, the easier it is for us to read what's there. Figure out what needs to be there and stick to that.

The panel is a two dimensional image, but we can create the illusion of space by working in three levels: Foreground, middle-ground, and background. The foreground is that which is closest to us, the reader. The back ground is the farthest from us and the objects in the foreground. It's sometimes good to use the foreground for items we want the reader's attention drawn to. The background becomes a place for action to take place. The middle ground is anything that happens in between

It's an extremely bad idea to have multiple actions taking place in a panel, unless you want two levels of story telling to occur at the same time. But people tend to be confused when too much is happening in a panel. You can use the foreground to focus on actions dealing with the main characters in these scenes, and the background for things they are either unaware of or actions drawing their attention.

The couple in the foreground get our attention, because they are closer to us. We can read their dialog. The changing scene in the background with the big man drawing closer gets our attention next. We know he's coming toward the couple before they do. This makes for a suspenseful sequence.

Some writers make the mistake of trying to show multiple actions in a panel to advance their story faster. They'll have character A punching character B in the foreground, while character C shoots character D in the background and character F is in the middle ground talking about how important it is to understand other people's feelings while character G accompanies him on the violin.

This is ill advised because the panel becomes cluttered

with all those figures, and it does a disservice to the action. Action reads better when each shot is clear and simple. Too many distractions slows down the pace of the scene. When you want to slow down the reading time, complexity does the trick. So does a lot of copy. But in the case of action, you want it to be clear and simple because that's more exciting.

When you write a panel it's a good idea to tell the artist only what they need to know in a clear and concise manner. Too many words describing a scene, or too many objects to be drawn, will turn the artist off. You want them to be inspired, so make their job easy and give them room to be creative. Never demand things from the artist, always be polite and ask. If something needs to be in that shot, make it clear to them that it's important. But cut to the chase and avoid boring them. You want them to find the story exciting when they read it the first time.

When you have scenes with lots of characters, keep the number of characters in a panel to a bare minimum. That is, unless you're requesting an establishing shot of a group. In that case, give them a big panel or a page to do it in. People's bodies take up a lot of room in a panel. Dialog usually has to go in there, so you're going to need all the space you can get.

Crowd scenes are something artists *really* hate to draw. If you must have a crowd scene, or show an army approaching, don't be surprised if they cheat and use some trick to avoid drawing all those figures. Don't ask for a crowd scene unless you really need it.

It's also a good idea to request no more than five or six panels to a page, maximum. The more room the artist has, the more freedom they have to draw things into the shot. They don't like doing seven or eight panel pages if they can help it.

An exception to this rule is pages with a lot of talking head shots. Those don't require so much work. But you still need room for copy. Always be aware of the need for copy.

When two characters are talking to each other in the same panel, the character who speaks first needs to be on the left side. We read from left to right, so the first balloon has to be on the left, over the first character. A lot of artists, even experienced ones, either don't know this rule or forget to do it. Make sure it's pointed out to them if you switch the speakers.

For example, let's say in panel one you have Joe Smith talking to John Q. Public. Joe speaks first, then John Q replies. The next panel is a close up of Joe's face as he says something. Then panel three has John Q speaking to Joe. We went from a panel where Joe Blow was the first speaker to a panel where John Q. Public talks first. A lot of artists will draw panel three exactly like panel one, with some minor variations. They'll forget the rule that the character who speaks first must stand on the left. So don't forget to remind them.

If only one person is speaking in a panel, then it doesn't matter. But if two people are talking, this is a rule to remember.

Panels come in all shapes and sizes. There are three basic shapes. The "box", which is generally square. The "flapjack", which is a long, shallow rectangle. The "silo" which is a vertical flapjack that runs up the side of the page from top to bottom.

The silo is great for introducing a character because you can easily get a full figure shot of them. When characters are introduced, it's important that we clearly see what they look like so we'll know them in later panels. The flapjack is mainly used to show head and shoulder shots of people talking. Or to show a panorama view of a scene. It's also good for POV shots. Everything else is generally well serviced by the box.

Odd shaped panels like circle and triangle shapes are design elements that an artist is best equipped to deal with. In general, they are not a good idea, simply because your goal is to tell a clear and concise story. When panels are misshapen it's often difficult to determine which one you're supposed to read first.

The same rule applies to panels that cross pages. These go from one page to the next and are hard to follow. People are used to reading all the panels on a page before looking at the next page. If you cross pages with panels, they have to consciously make the adjustment. And then go back to "normal" reading when they get past this section. That is very distracting, and distraction is something to avoid. It's better not to do them. I've never seen it done in a way that wouldn't have worked better if they stayed on their own page.

Double page spreads are panels that take up two whole pages. These should be reserved for highly critical shots that involve complexity or serious emotional impact. They should not go to prosaic scenes or incidents that could have been handled in a splash page or less. The audience views these things as filler when they're wasted on unimportant shots. When they think you're adding filler, they start thinking the story is junk.

When describing the panel to the artist, it's a good idea to keep your panel descriptions clean and concise. Tell them exactly what they need to know, but don't go into excessive detail. There are some writers famous for the detail they put into a panel, but they usually have something to say that's relevant. Personally, I don't think it's a good idea to distract the artist with too many things.

When they draw the page they need to look at your panel description and be able to get the gist of it quickly. If there are too many words, they may forget some element you described and will forget to draw it.

You also don't want to burden them with too many details, because your job is to inspire them not to order them. You are giving the artist the information they need to translate a cut of time into an illustration. You want them to be interested and excited. You want them to show a love for every line and texture. Because we're dealing with a medium where art is a major selling point. The art has to not only tell the story, it has to sell the book.

REMEMBER: Make every shot count and make them clear.

SCENES

Now that we understand polarity, we can talk about scenes. Scenes are the smallest component of the story, after panels (if you are doing comics). They are like miniature stories within the story. And they should follow the same basic formula of story structure. A>B<C.

A is the hero of the scene. B is the conflict/villain standing in the way. C is the Grail.

If we look at the one act comic strip as an example. We see that one character is usually talking to another character. Character A wants something, be it information, attention, money, etc. Character B is always going to resist in some way. The punchline of a comic strip is how they resist. Usually it's with some joke that has a negative effect on character A. So we see polarity in action. Comic strips almost always start positive and end negative because humor is usually found in pain.

A scene should follow the rules of the one act story. The ending should have some kind of punchline at the end. A pay off. This gives the scene it's own premise, which gives it weight.

This applies to prose or screenplays scenes. They may be short but in their own way they are like mini stories. Basically one act plays. The scene will advance your story (unless its wasted). But it should have its own internal logic and point.

The average scene in a comic takes up one or two pages. The one page scene is a good size because you can set up a tight series of panels to get to a quick punch at the end. But when you need a long scene you can add pages or panels until you accomplish the length you want.

In prose, a chapter might make up a whole scene. Though many chapters are made up of scenes and form a sequence. It depends on what is being attempted. The principals are the same, as they are in a film where a scene can be less than a minute or more.

Whatever medium you are working in, the Audience should have a sense that this next scene is somehow linked to the events of the storyline in a logical progression from the last scene. Otherwise it's rather jarring to make a jump from one into something completely different in tone and pace.

Another thing to remember when doing one page scenes in comics is that even numbered pages are what you see when you turn a page, odd numbered pages are the page you have to turn. Therefore, the last panel on an odd numbered page can be used to set up a surprise when the reader turns the page. The only thing that can screw you up are the advertisements. You may have to find out where they normally get placed or ask that the ads don't effect something you've set up. They can usually play around with the ads to accommodate the needs of your story.

The panel count to a scene should be based on the type of actions taking place. The kinetic principle holds that the shorter the scene, the faster the pace. If you want to slow things down, add more panels and make scenes longer. By the same token, double page spreads are very static to look at, even when they are action shots. A choreographed series of panels showing action cinematically flows in a more exciting manner.

REMEMBER: Scenes are like miniature stories. Make them end with a pay off.

SEQUENCES

Sequences are a section of the story, composed of scenes, relating a major incident in the act. In THE GODFATHER, the first sequence is the Wedding. It's composed of myriad scenes which show different things happening at the Wedding of Vito Corleone's daughter. The second sequence is the Hollywood Deal. Tom Hagan goes to Hollywood to try to convince a producer that he must hire an actor friend of the Godfather's. The producer refuses and wakes up the next morning with a severed horse's head lying between his legs. These sequences tell us a section of the story which are building toward act's climax. They serve to narrate a progression of events that the scenes have constructed.

Sequences are generally thematically linked. They form a bigger picture than the scene. The scene is only showing us one event that happened. A sequence tells us how a series of events formed a greater whole and this is the end result.

Like scenes and acts, the sequence builds toward a climax. It has it's own resolution. It follows the general formula of A>B<C, as well. The resolution of a sequence is related to its importance in the chain of events. If it's the last sequence in an act, then it ends with the Turning Point scene of that act, or its climax.

Just as scenes should follow a logical order, sequences need to construct the story in a pattern that makes sense. Some stories tell sequences out of order, but this is done to fill in the story different parts at a time until the whole picture is complete. If a sequence is something that takes place out of the continuity of the previous and following sequence, you may want to put it somewhere else. Remember that you are building towards something and the choice of appropriate scenes and sequences are essential.

REMEMBER: Sequences build toward the act's climax. Order them well.

BEGINNINGS

"Grab 'em by the throat and never let 'em go." Billy Wilder

How you begin any story is important. You have to interest people from the start. There's a good chance that some potential reader might pick up your book in the store, read the first page, and decide if it looks interesting. You have to nail them on the spot. You have to make them go: "I gotta buy this!"

In prose it's best to find an engaging opening. Famed crime writer Elmore Leonard said don't open with weather. Stanley Kubrick picked the Stephen King novel *The Shining* after throwing away over 100 books because the first sentence grabbed him. "Jack Torrance thought: Officious little prick." And he kept reading. You have to catch people right away. Some of the most famous books in literature start with a memorable sentence. "It was the best of times, it was the worst of times." Is one of my favorites from Charles Dickens *A Tale of Two Cities*. Film or television start off best with something that captivates you.

In comics, when you sit down to think what that first page is going to show, think of it as the money shot. That first page has the potential to sell your book. It also sets the tone. It can also be used to establish the premise or a theme. In FORREST GUMP, the first image we saw was a floating feather, which was a metaphor for one of story's themes. Forrest Gump was sort of blown around on the winds of fate and landed in some amazing adventures.

If you do a splash page, you should try to think of an original and interesting opening. One they will pay attention to. Jack Kirby was great with those back in the sixties. When I was a kid, I would grab his comics off the rack just to see what the opening shot was. He always came up with something that made you go "Wow!"

As a rule of thumb, your story should begin in motion. Events should be taking place which are going to upset the balance of your Hero's life. As we discussed earlier, the first act is going to be relatively short. And the turning point of the first act is going to throw the protagonist headlong, directly at the conflict. So you might as well get the ball rolling from panel one. Start in medias res. Use action, conflict, mystery or humor to get us interested in what is going on. Make the audience wonder and care who the people are and what is going to happen to them. Hit the ground running.

It's not a bad idea to show the Hero's life is already in a state of flux. Either he's between jobs, his wife hates him, there's no money coming in and he might have to move, something that tells us he's ready for a change of some kind. Change is what life is all about and stories are metaphors for life. Remember?

Having the balance of things upset at the beginning gives it inertia from the start. You can then propel the story further along with every panel or scene there after.

In monthly comics it's hard to have the character's life in upheaval at the beginning of every story, so many writers try to do it by leaving cliff hangers at the end of the previous issue. This keeps the momentum going, but if done improperly it can also ruin the energy of the story. If you start out with a slam bang at the beginning you have to top it by the end. There's no way to keep doing this month after month, so it's not wise to fall into that trap.

Normally, the way to get momentum going in the beginning is with the Trigger Event. Which just happens to be our next chapter.

THE TRIGGER EVENT

This is one of the most critical things a story needs. It's an event that sets the story in motion. Until this event happens, your characters are just muddling through life as they normally do. The Trigger Event kicks the plot into first gear. Now you're moving in a *direction.*

Think of a story as a section of your character's life, which has been edited down to the most interesting parts. We live from day to day, trying to achieve certain objectives. Things happen to us that sometimes changes our plans. And sometimes these events set us on a different path than the one we were on.

That's what the trigger does. It sets your character on a path with destiny. The destiny you've chosen for him at the end of the story. Until the trigger he was headed in the "normal" direction his life was taking, whatever that may be. He had a goal in sight or he was doing a daily routine and everything was hunky dory. More or less.

But then the trigger event came along and totally screwed up *everything.* It has radically upset the life of the hero whether he realizes it or not. The trigger can either have a positive or negative effect on the hero's life at first, but it must be dynamic. It must radically alter the status quo in a way that will take a lot of doing to change.

A story needs to have movement. It needs to propel the Audience forward at a pace where they won't be distracted or have their mind wander. A story also needs direction, and the trigger gives the story the initial direction it needs.

In a story you have two opposing forces, the Hero and the Villain. Both will be at odds over some issue central to the story. That issue will usually be the Grail. The trigger event signals when these two forces first begin to be in opposition to each other. It may not be apparent immediately to some of the characters that this is happening, but the trigger serves as the catalyst to make the story come about.

Let's look at a few famous movies to see some examples of a trigger event.

E.T.: The UFO that brought E.T. to earth has left without him. He's stranded on an alien world. The UFO was seen by some government men, including a man with keys on his belt (the story's Villain). The man with the keys senses E.T.'s presence and gives chase. E.T. runs until he reaches the safety of the garden shed where he'll eventually meet Henry, the central Hero of the story.

STAR WARS: A NEW HOPE: A spaceship carrying Princess Leia and her two droids is captured by the Empire. Darth Vader, the main Villain, shows up to oversee the operation. The two droids escape to the planet below, where they inevitably meet Luke Skywalker, the main Hero. Luke's Aunt and Uncle is killed when he tries to return the droids. That sets him on the path of the jedi.

SPECTRE: James Bond (the main Hero) is assigned to kill a terrorist in Mexico City. He finds a ring on the body and discovers it has traces of DNA from previous criminals he's killed. This leads him to Mr. White, a former person of interest to tells him of this criminal organization and its mysterious leader. Bond's pursuit of this organization takes him to the author of all his pain.

DIE HARD: John McClane, a New York Cop (the main Hero) shows up at his wife's office party and goes into her office to make a phone call. Shortly thereafter, a band of criminals (lead by the Villain) show up and take people hostage at the party.

ALIEN: The spaceship Nostromo gets orders to land on an alien planet, where the crew (the Heroes) will come into contact with an alien species (the Villain) which will try to kill them all.

Did you notice something about all these trigger events? Either the Villain, the Hero, or both were introduced in them. This is important, because every story will be about these two forces coming into opposition. You want to make it clear who these characters are and what place do they take in the scheme of things.

So the Trigger Event not only starts the ball rolling in a certain direction, but it serves to give the audience a sense of who's who and what's about to go down.

In the case of *E.T.*, we know right away that the alien is in trouble and that he's hunted. That his only hope is to be taken in by someone who will protect him. This is a great trigger incident because it immediately gives you a clear sense of where the story is going and raises a strong question.

Star Wars: A New Hope also does a good job of establishing the nature of the Villain and his relationship to the Heroes of the story, even though we don't see Luke Skywalker till a little while later.

In *Spectre*, James Bond's discovery of a ring is a crucial lead that opens the door to solving a host of mysteries that have been plaguing him.

Placement of the Trigger Event

The Trigger Event should be placed close to the beginning of the story. You might even want to make it the first scene. The only real reason to hold off using it right away is when you need to set up some backstory so that everything makes sense. For example, in *The Godfather*, the trigger doesn't happen until after the large wedding sequence. In fact, it doesn't happen until after the infamous horse head scene. The wedding scene establishes all the main characters of the story and sets up a backstory, showing the Godfather's relationship with his community, his power over others, and the nature of what he is. The wedding sequence also establishes his son, Michael, who is the Hero of the story. We even wait until after the Hollywood sequence before we get to the Trigger. The Hollywood sequence demonstrates Godfather Vito Corleone's influence and power via the infamous "horse head" scene. Before then, we only heard second hand stories about the Godfather's power. Now we've seen it in action. We see the fear he creates in others. We are led to believe that someone would have to be crazy to ever think of messing with this dude. This is all a set up for the Turning Point of the first act.

The Trigger Event is the scene where Vito rejects Virgil Pollazo's offer to join him in the drug trade. By refusing Pollazo, the Godfather has created a powerful enemy who will attempt to have him assassinated at the Turning Point of the first act. Since Michael is the hero of the movie, the attempted murder of his father sets him on the path to become the new Godfather.

So, sometimes it's necessary to wait before you use the trigger. Sometimes you need to get to know the victims first. But in any event, it must be somewhere in the first quarter of your story.

The Trigger Event can sometimes be in the backstory, rather than a scene in the first act. In *Watchmen* it was in the murder of the Comedian, which we only see the aftermath of in the beginning. This is because *Watchmen* is a mystery and it would give away the story's big twist if we knew who killed the Comedian. This technique of placing the Trigger in the backstory is common in the mystery and crime genres. The hero of the story is arguably Rorschach who is the person who tries to solve the mystery of who killed the Comedian to the end.

RISING ACTION

When a story begins we usually enter into a series of events known as *rising action*. These scenes establish the momentum of the story from the beginning. They are made up of decisions, characters' flaws and background circumstances that together create turns and twists leading to a climax. The events in this part of the story are a logical progression of what was set up at the start. We've met some characters. We've been given a rough idea what they want to do. Now they are setting out to accomplish their goals. And naturally, these goals just happen to be in direct opposition to what some other characters want. Or, if it's a story about internal conflict, what the hero's inner self wants.

The rising action serves to build the story's energy toward the first big reversal. The Turning Point. In the midst of all this is Trigger Event, which is the force that starts the whole ball rolling toward the inevitable climax.

The rising action phase of the story needs to be really compelling because this will determine if you've hooked the reader or not. If the audience isn't hooked in the beginning of the story, they may put it down to read later. So already, you've bored them. The story isn't interesting enough for them to keep reading.

If that's the case, you're in trouble.

Take a good hard look at the beginning of your story. Is it really exciting? Is it really interesting? Don't think that some guy blasting a machine gun at us is exciting on its own. It's not something we haven't seen before. Exciting isn't just action. Exciting is something that sucks us in. That draws our attention. It can be a naked body. It can be an unusual sight. It could be a revealed secret. Or...it can even be a shot of action. But we'd better care about who is involved in that action. Remember the rules of conflict.

The rising action scenes also establish the mood of the story. As we discussed before, once the mood is set, you have to stick with it until the next act. And even then, don't make the mistake of confusing the audience. There must be a pervasive mood to every story.

You should also use the action to tell us who the characters are and why they are in opposition to each other. In the first act we need to know who the hero is, what he's after, and why he's not able to get it. Who the villain is and why they're in the way should also be clear.

When introducing the villain, make sure his first scene is really interesting. The villain is the linchpin of the story. He has to grab the audience's attention in a big way. More on that later.

REMEMBER: Start with momentum and keep us interested from the first shot.

THE STORY'S QUESTION

When the Trigger Event takes place, it should immediately create the following question in the Audience's mind.

"How does this end?"

Your Trigger Event needs to be interesting enough to make the Audience wonder how the hero is going to win. Or at least make people wonder where this is going, in a positive way. After all, the last thing you want is people to feel is indifference. Boredom is the enemy of all stories. Interest doesn't have to be suspenseful. Comedy's do it by amusing you with a set up. Mysteries intrigue you. Romances entice you. But every one needs to make you wonder what happens next, If the Audience doesn't care, that's not good.

The Trigger should provoke an image in the mind of the Audience of what the final confrontation will be, even though you may have other plans. It gives them something to stick around for.

What the Trigger does is make clear to the audience that after this event, nothing is going to be the same. The Hero will not be able to just mosey along as he always has. The T.E. has screwed him major. It has put him in a situation that he is going to have to figure a way out of, even if he doesn't know it yet.

Let's examine a few examples for clarification.

DIE HARD: The trigger forces John McClane to fight the criminals who've invaded the building. He could have just surrendered right away like the other people did, but because he was a cop and a man of honor, he had to do the right thing. Either way, he was not going to walk away from this story without some major changes to his life. If he didn't fight the criminals, his self respect and his relationship with his estranged wife and kids might have suffered.

GLADIATOR: General Maximus of Ancient Rome (Russell Crowe) is the favorite of the Emperor Marcus Aurelius. But when the emperor's son, Commodus (Joaquin Phoenix) murders him, Maximus is sentenced to death for not supporting the new Emperor. Maximus escapes death but ends up a slave in the arenas where he will face Commodus again. The trigger raises a huge question for Maximus is taken from great heights to extreme lows and you wonder how he will get through it all.

THE WIZARD OF OZ: The trigger event in this story is when Mrs. Gulch shows up at Dorothy's house and takes Toto away to be killed. This forces Dorothy into despair, motivating her to run away when Toto escapes. By running away she ends up in the house when the Tornado comes and whisks her and Toto off to the land of Oz. But the scene where she runs away is not the Trigger. It is the Turning point at the end of Act One.

GRAVITY: Sandra Bullock's astronaut character is on a space mission with George Clooney and another astronaut when a damaged satellite destroys their space station. This trigger event leaves Clooney and Bullock with the clear hopeless mission to survive in outer space with no rescue possible. How can they do it? That is the big story question created by the trigger event.

As we see in these examples, the trigger forces the hero to make a choice of some kind, which will affect the outcome of the story. The choice is not always immediate. The choice will often have to be made after the turning point of the first act.

The choice which will eventually be *forced* upon the hero by the Trigger is what raises the story question in the audience's mind. They immediately begin to see what the possible outcomes are, and this is the start of a phenomena known as the "Audience Bond".

The Audience Bond

Once you have the audience wondering what's going to happen next, you have created an empathy for the Hero. This bond between the audience and your characters is critical to the success of your work.

Just as we discussed in the choice section, people respond to gambles. High stakes with large pay offs and consequences attached. Not knowing which is the right choice is what makes it exciting. When you force the Hero to make hard choices, you give the audience the means to feel right along with the Hero as he has to make his decision. You've created a bond between the Audience and the Hero. It's critical that you don't blow it once you've done this.

You can blow it by having the character make stupid choices for no good reason. If the character acts in an unsympathetic manner, we lose empathy for them.

Another mistake is to use cheap surprise, which is having illogical or unbelievable things happen at random for shock value. In one bad suspense movie whose title escapes me at the moment, the Heroine hears a noise in her kitchen late at night. She's afraid a killer is stalking her. For some reason she goes in the kitchen with the lights off and opens a cupboard. SURPRISE! Her *cat* leaps out at her! It's never explained why the cat would be in the cupboard with the doors closed. Events like that aren't credible and they will annoy your audience.

The Audience Bond is an important thing to sustain. It's essential to making your story work, because maintaining a grasp on the audience's attention is the difference between being remembered and being discarded.

REMEMBER: The Trigger Event gets your story moving. Make sure it evokes the story question.

TURNING POINTS

After the trigger event comes the turning point. The trigger is usually somewhere between the beginning and the middle of the first act. The turning point is a major plot twist that throws us into the next act, full speed ahead.

There is a Turning Point at the end of *every* act. It serves as the *act's climax*. Its purpose is to twist the plot in a different direction than where it was going before. This gives the story more momentum. It also makes it more surprising.

To use our desert road analogy, if you're driving down a road that goes it a straight line on a flat terrain, there aren't going to be too many surprises up ahead. You'll be able to see things coming from miles away. And so would the Audience. A story shouldn't be predictable. We always assume the hero is going to win, but the question should be "How?". The answer to that question needs to be a surprise.

The Turning Point twists that road so the audience's and the hero's expectations are thrown off balance. We now have to figure out what to do next. This helps solidify the Audience Bond because the Audience is now involved with the Hero's problems.

In *The Godfather*, the Trigger was Vito Corleone's refusal to help the crime lord Sollazo with his drug business. This led to the Turning Point of the first act, which was the attempted assassination on Vito. Now Vito is in the hospital and we're not sure if he'll live or die. This forces the Hero of the story, Michael Corleone, to get involved in the family business. Up until that time, he avoided any involvement. Now, by involving himself in the underworld, Michael Corleone becomes a changed

94

man. No longer an innocent, his hands become stained with blood.

The Trigger throws the conflict and the Hero into a collision course. The Turning Point is where they first collide. This has to be a major train wreck, folks. It's got to seriously upset the Audience's expectations of the story's direction.

The Turning Point needs to be a logical result of the Trigger Event. The Audience must feel this was bound to happen as a result of the Trigger. But even though it should be logical, the Turning Point should also be surprising. It should make the Audience get excited and interested in what's going to happen next.

Act climaxes tend to be the longest scenes in a story, and the tension in these scenes is the most extreme. So when you construct your Turning Point, remember to make them exciting as they throw the story in a new direction. These scenes are crucial to keeping the story moving.

REMEMBER: Turning Points throw the story in a new, but logical direction.

PROGRESSIVE COMPLICATIONS

This is the meat of the story. This is where a large part of your creativity comes into play because here is where you heat up the conflict and keep the flames stoked high. Without conflict, you have a cold story. A dull story. A story people are not going to care about.

In life, the things that are worth having are the things we have to struggle for. Nothing that comes easy is precious to us. But when we fight for something, it's like gold. This is a truism every member of your audience can relate to, which is why the conflict is one of the most important components of the story.

When we go about our day-to-day affairs we take the path of least resistance. When we walk to the store, we almost always take the same route. This is the way human beings function. But it's all pretty boring. It's not the stuff of fiction.

In a story you have to make your hero's journey as interesting and exciting as possible. The greater the conflict, the greater the hero, the greater the audience's interest level. Progressive complication deals with putting pressure on your character in a way the Audience can relate to. This is done by playing with the technique known as Reversal. Reversals are the walls that spring up between expectation and result.

When you take that walk to the store, something could happen along the way unlike anything that has ever happened all the millions of times you took that same walk. And it could prevent you from getting to the store by taking the path of least resistance. In other words, you have hit a wall. A complication. Now you have to find a way around that wall.

Your Hero is going after the Grail of the story. They

need to go after it in a relentless way. They will scale any wall, climb any mountain to get there. And you need to demonstrate that. The value of the Grail is measured by the risk the Hero takes to reach it.

So back to our analogy about walking to the store. Let's say a carton of milk in the store is the Grail. The Hero's name is Kyle. Kyle is having a major hunger for some Capt. Crunch cereal. He goes to the fridge and finds he's out of milk. So he heads out and walks down Sycamore street toward the convenience store two blocks away. Suddenly, there's a terrible earthquake and a huge flaming crevice opens between Kyle and the distant store. He can't go down Sycamore, which is the route he always takes. So he turns down Willow, a side street that connects to Maple Blvd, which will take him south, the direction of the store.

But, because of the quake, police and fire trucks have shown up and are blocking off Maple Blvd. So now Kyle has no choice. He must try another route. He turns and walks down Willow in the opposite direction until he gets to Pine Street. He takes Pine to Oak street and cuts back up Sycamore, on the other side of the crevice. He sees the store in the distance. But as he walks down the street he sees a mob of looters running amok ahead. Kyle's on the only street he can take now. So he decides to go ahead and take his chances. He's got to have that milk! As he walks toward the store, a band of thugs come up and try to rob him.

Kyle rushes them like a running back, breaking through their line. He knocks them aside. But one of them has a gun and starts shooting. Kyle dives behind a parked car. The gunman shoots at the car. The gas tank blows. Kyle rolls away as flames and shrapnel go flying. A jagged chunk of hot metal skewers the ground where he just was half a second ago.

The gunman comes after him, taking aim. Kyle grabs the shrapnel and throws it. It slices into the looter's chest, stabbing him in the right lung. He goes down, gurgling blood. His gun falls to the grass. His friends see this and come after Kyle, screaming with rage. Kyle grabs the fallen man's gun and makes a run for it. They start shooting at him.

Kyle spins, fires, and the looters go down one by one. Kyle is now only 10 yards from the store. But the police heard the shooting and pull into the parking lot, sirens blaring. They see Kyle has a gun and jump out of their cars, ready to shoot, ordering him to stop.

Kyle ignores them, runs into the store. The cops start firing. Bullets shatter the store windows, hitting product on the shelves. Soda bottles explode. Cartons of cereal go flying, spritzing Cherrios. Kyle rushes to the back, but a Pakistani clerk tries to block his way, jabbering in some foreign tongue.

Kyle throws a punch, it connects with the man's nose. The clerk goes flying back into the slush machine. He hits his head, bounces forward, falling unconscious to the floor. Cherry slush dribbles onto his back.

Kyle spots the milk just behind the glass door in the refrigerated section. He makes for it. Just then, police enter the store, firing away. Bullets shatter the glass and milk cartons spray their contents. White fountains of the stuff splatters on the floor. Kyle tries to avoid the bullets, slips and falls on his back. Glass shards from the case slice into his flesh and he screams as--

What you just read is a series of progressive complications. If Kyle had just turned around and walked to a different store in the opposite direction, it would've been boring. Or he might have ran into a friend and they would get into a conversation that would throw the plot in another direction. But instead he walked in the direction of the conflict and here is where our story was born. Of course, you have to make sure it was a logical thing for Kyle to do. Otherwise the audience is going to say, "Why didn't he just go to another store?" So maybe we could add a line that this particular store has a special brand of milk he can't buy anywhere else. The only brand he finds acceptable.

Notice how each progressive complication was a logical extension of the last one. That's how they need to work.

When Kyle went around the crevice, he encountered a road block set up because of the crevice caused by the earthquake. And as a result of this earthquake, people started looting. Kyle had to deal with the looters in order to go in the only direction left to take. And because he fought the looters he drew the attention of the police. And because the police fired at him, the milk was shot up, sprayed on the floor, and he slipped on it, falling on the glass. Now he's lying on a slippery floor, with glass stuck in his back, and a bunch of cops are coming for him.

Every time Kyle went to take an action, something else came up to make his life more difficult. Each time, the stakes were raised. This makes the story more exciting as we read along. It also makes the Grail seem like an object of great value, even though in this case it was only a carton of milk.

Each time Kyle has a choice. He can stop, give up, or he can press on. His determination is what inspires our empathy. We can relate to life throwing road blocks in our path. It happens to us all the time, even if it isn't as dramatic as the story you just read. Empathy makes us become involved with Kyle's struggle. We live along side him every step of the way. We feel it when he falls to the floor and glass cuts him.

Every time Kyle choose to press on, he's passed a point of no return. Especially as we get closer to the grail. Once he started fighting with those looters, he couldn't turn around and go home. Now the police are after him. Now he's in serious trouble. How you solve this crisis is the climax of the story, which we will deal with shortly.

The Trigger Event in this story was Kyle going to the fridge and finding he was out of milk. The Turning Point was the earthquake. What followed then was a series of progressive complications. This formed the bulk of the action. In a bigger story we would have scenes of dialog, perhaps internal monologues where Kyle debated what he should do. There might be details of the scene described. All of this would flesh out the world and the characters. But when you boil things down to the conflict, this is what you see. One progressive complication after the other. Each slowing down the Hero as he tries to reach the Grail. Each raising the stakes so it gets harder and more frenzied every step of the way. And finally you reach a crisis situation where it's do or die. This is the point of no return. Either the hero wins the Grail or he loses big time. It should never be easy at the end. The end should be the toughest part of the story.

When creating Progressive Complications think about all the possible outcomes that could happen when the hero takes an action. Then separate the most surprising and believable outcomes and choose one. Beware of the absurd, unless you are trying to do that.

This outcome will always force the hero to make a choice. How clever your hero is in dealing with that choice defines his cool factor. When he deals with the reversal and moves on, there should be repercussions that follow. And those repercussions will create a new surprise for him to deal with.

And each complication should make the stakes higher and higher until your hero is facing the ultimate challenge. This ultimate challenge is called the Crisis. And it will decide how good the ending of your story is going to be. You need to build toward a *real* crisis.

Whatever you do, don't have the Hero retry the same tactics after they failed. When a hero attempts to repeat previous actions which have proved to be fruitless, it makes the Audience feel the hero is treading water and the story is going nowhere. Besides, the definition of insanity is trying the same thing over and over again expecting a different result. Your character should not come off as crazy or foolish unless you want to make a point about it.

You start encountering the laws of diminishing returns when you repeat experiences in a story. And these don't have to be literally the same. If they even smack of being similar you run the risk of boring the Audience. So be careful.

It's also important to try to hit the first three levels of conflict if possible. Internal, Personal, and Societal. This makes the intensity of the story all that much greater. When you have a character with inner conflicts who is also having problems at home and with his boss, it creates a more complex story.

The example of progressive complications we used was the kind found in an action story. But if you want to see progressive complications in a suspense film, I highly recommend *North by Northwest*. If you want to see progressive complications in a comedy, try *Ruthless People*. Progressive complications will work in any genre. That's the beauty of it.

When you get to the end of the second act, or the final scene of the progressive complication stage, this scene must end down. It will, of course, be a Turning Point scene. This scene propels the story into the Crisis. You can't enter a Crisis on an up note. You have to end down. And the harder, the better.

REMEMBER: Each progressive complication raises the stakes. Build toward the crisis.

CRISIS

"The event that occurs at the second act curtain triggers the end of the movie." Billy Wilder

Also known as "The Critical Juncture" or "The Moment of Truth". It is often confused with the Climax, because it often is in the Climactic scene. But I want to separate it for a moment to explain what it is. It often takes place right before the Climax. The crisis comes right after the last Turning Point in the story. It's the Crisis that precipitates the Climax. Your whole story leads up to this point. The level of intensity of your Crisis has a major impact on how good your ending is going to be.

The Crisis is the last possible situation the Hero can deal with. By this time, the Hero has passed the point of no return. All the forces of the Villain and the Antagonists are against him at their utmost strength. If the Hero fails to deal with the Crisis, he loses the Grail and the story has a negative ending. If he wins, the ending is probably going to be positive, unless you set it up otherwise.

During the progressive complication stage of the story, the Hero makes a series of choices which leads to one complication after another. The conflict heats up until it reaches this boiling point. Now your Hero is in a do or die situation. He *must* win. If he fails, all is lost. He's exhausted every possible alternative.

The Crisis can be part of the Climax, but when the Crisis involves a decision, you can place it a scene or two before the Climax so the audience is kept in suspense, wondering if the Hero made the right decision. It also makes the decision seem more complex.

But the decision should not come during the crisis when you use this technique. It should be a static moment. So place it in the next scene, and better if it's demonstrated rather than said.

At any rate, the decision made as a result of the crisis is the deepest look we get into the character's psyche. This is the moment of truth. How they choose tells us who they really are. What they are really made of. This scene should produce meaningful emotion in the audience. This is achieved by making the crisis is critically important on as many levels of the conflict as possible.

Here's a great example of the Crisis from the classic Western, *The Wild Bunch.* The Wild Bunch are a group of outlaws who find themselves in Mexico where they just made a deal with a revolutionary general. The Wild Bunch had to deal with all kinds of trials and tribulations to give the general what he wanted and now they've been reward. They have the money they wanted and can leave, but there is one problem. The General is keeping on of their men. He wants to torture him to death because he wanted to protect his village. The Wild Bunch make a decision, facing certain death they know they can't leave one of their men behind. So they face the General and his army in what is sure to be a battle to the death. It ;s the crisis point in the story. But not the climax. That comes next.

Meaning produces emotion. Especially when pressure is extreme. By heating up the conflict on the internal, personal, and social levels you can create intense meaning for the crisis. And this can produce a significant emotional response in the Audience.

The other means of achieving this, which is related to the levels of conflict, is through *story values*. A subject we will explore in detail later. The key thing you have to remember to do is bring all the levels of conflict to a head at the same time and find a way to solve them all in the climax. This way, the power of the story is released in one final explosion.

And then your Audience will hear sweet music.

REMEMBER: The Crisis is the litmus test for your character. Make it meaningful.

CLIMAX

Our friends the Ancient Greeks, called the Climax the "ladder." It's because we've climbed all the rungs of the story and reached the top. The Climax is where the Hero comes face to face with the Villain and fights him to the finish. This is the make or break scene of your story. It's the pay off for the whole shebang. If you were to break down the effort that goes into a story, 75% should go into the story and 25% should go into the ending. The ending makes a lasting impression on the Audience. If it's a weak ending, people will walk away generally unimpressed.

You should try to wrap up the climax with one action that solves everything. Because all the forces should have come to a head. It should all be down to one act of will. One act that will either defeat the Villain or make the Hero lose if it fails.

This creates immense tension right at the moment of truth.

The Audience wants emotional satisfaction. You need to give them what they want, but not like they expect. Endings need to have an element of surprise to be satisfying. If they end exactly the way people expect, they're going to think you didn't try very hard. And then they're going to be more critical of the story.

Try to look at the Climax as a cross roads. The hero has a choice of directions he can take during the climax. Only you, the writer, know where those diverse roads lead. You decide which one the Hero chooses and which fate awaits him at the end.

One way to guarantee the Audience will get turned off is by taking the Climax out of the Hero's hands. When you let someone else win the Grail or solve the problem, you steal all the energy from the climax. You are saying that the whole story leading up to this point was irrelevant because the Hero wasn't really needed. That is probably one of the worst things you can do in fiction. It's called a "deus ex machina" ending, which means "God in a Machine". In Ancient Greece, a lot of bad plays had gods showing up at the end the climax, waving their hand, solving all the problems in the story. Audiences hated it then and they hate it now. Even if you *don't* use gods.

There is one exception that was worked in a major movie. That is the end of *Raiders of the Lost Ark.* Indiana Jones actually failed in that movie to rescue the ark. But it didn't matter. God literally fixed things. But that is not a recommended solution to a story.

Audiences nowadays have seen so many movies, read so many comics and novels that they are jaded. They want some bang for their buck and you need to wrack your brain to provide some.

It's a good idea to use a visual that some how represents the premise at the end of the Climax. This is known as a "Key Image" and it can create a powerful, lasting moment that stays with the Audience after they finish your tale.

For example, in CITIZEN KANE the final image is a shot of a child's sled burning in the flames with the logo ROSEBUD on it. It answers the question of the story, what is Rosebud. It also represents the premise, which is: "Take away a boy's childhood and you end up with a childish man." The sled represents his lost childhood going up in flames.

A large portion of the Audiences expectations and satisfaction comes from the end of the climax, so make it worth the price of admission. It's the most important scene in the whole story.

Let's go back to Kyle for an example of Climax. When

we left off, Kyle was lying on the floor of the convenience store, with glass sticking into his back. And cops were converging on him. This is a crisis situation. How does he get out of it? Let's find out...

The glass is grinding into his back, jarring Kyle with pain. The gun is slippery in his hand. Milk has sprayed all over him. The sound of the cops footsteps is get louder. Kyle knows they'll come around the shelves and see him any second. He starts to get up, but the milk soaked floor makes it hard. His back is in agony. What does he do? Should he give up or get that damned carton?

Kyle looks at the shattered case. One carton remains unscathed. He reaches for it. Gets it. Suddenly he feels renewed. Determination fills him from head to toe. He rams his body against the shelves as he hears the cops coming near.

An avalanche of cans hits them, they topple backward as Kyle leaps up and starts to shoot.

Klik klik klik

The gun's empty.

Kyle races for the exit, kicking a gun from a cop's hands before leaping over him. He clutches the milk carton like a football. The store's exit is the goal line. He's racing for it. The cop's partner tries to get up, but slips on the puddle of slush that's been growing on the floor like a B-movie monster. His shot goes wild and takes out several cartons of Camels near the cash register.

As Kyle rushes out the door, he hears sirens approaching. More heat! He dives in a nearby cop car and starts the engine. The two cops come running out as he shoves the transmission in reverse. They start firing at him. Bullets shatter the safety glass in the windshield, making it impossible to see. Kyle floors it and the car screeches backward, tires smoking like chimneys.

He swerves the car around and puts it in drive. He smashes his forearm into the windshield, knocking out the glass so he can see. Three cops cars are racing into the parking lot before him, blocking the exit. He floors it and spins the wheel, driving off the sidewalk onto the street. They give chase. He tries to turn left at the intersection, but two more cop cars and an ambulance are blocking that way, so he turns right.

Damn! The crevice is up ahead. No way over it. But the street behind him is full of cop cars!

No choice but to floor it. The ground has risen up on his side of the crevice, making it higher than the other side. As he rushes toward the crevice he sees the whole adventure flashing before his eyes. He sees himself falling into the crevice toward flames. Pitchfork wielding demons are waiting for him below with gleeful expressions on their evil faces. There's a second where he feels himself falling.

KATHUMP

He made it! The car made it across!

He looks in the rear view mirror. Cop cars are diving in the crevice. Others are trying to stop and end up crashing into each other. One car gets pushed in the hole by the one behind it.

Kyle makes for his apartment, laughing all the way home.

Of course, this was an absurdly overblown action story. I used the action motif to show the climax in its extreme. But you can do a great job with climaxes without having action. The film *Death and the Maiden* has a great climax with no action. Another good example is *Rear Window*. Study films for examples, rather than comics because most comics are bad examples of how to do things.

REMEMBER: The end of the Climax is the make or break scene in your story, in more ways than one.

RESOLUTION

Now your story is basically over and in this final scene you finish up the tale.

This is not a good place to wrap up plot threads. It looks clumsy if you do. Except if there is some kind of twist that your planning with one of the plot threads.

By and large, all questions raised by the story should have been answered by the time you reach this scene. Notice I don't say scenes. The Resolution should not be a sequence. Long resolutions make for boring ends to stories. How many movies have you seen where there was this long drawn out sequence at the end, after the Climax that bored you silly? *The Return of the King* had one that they mainly got away with because there was so many stories to tie up but not all people loved it.

As we discussed earlier, the Climax isn't called the climax for nothing. After a climax, are ready to leave the theater or close the book. The only kind of long resolution that people like is one that serves as a small, quiet mini story that brings an emotional sense of closure to the tale.

The Resolution can also be used to set up a sequel. You could use a twist ending that's a weaker punch than the end of the Climax, but which tells us that there's bound to be another. Examples of this kind of ending is where the Villain appears to have been killed, the Hero walks away, and the last shot is the Villain's hand moving or his eyes opening suddenly.

Many writers use these endings to say: "What you just saw was nothing. The best is yet to come." There is a problem with that kind of statement, obviously. You want people to like the story they just experienced and it may be really tough to out do what you just did. So be careful with your resolutions.

If you have a happy ending it's always good to end it with a warm feeling that makes them smile.

The great director Billy Wilder said it best: "The third act must build, build, build in tempo and action until the last event, and then—that's it. Don't hang around."

REMEMBER: Keep your resolutions short.

ENDINGS

"There is no real ending. It's just the place where you stop the story."
Frank Herbert

Resolutions are the ending of the story, even though the end of the Climax determines the outcome for the hero. The Resolution can put a spin on it that changes everything, however.

There are only three possible endings: Up, Down, and Ironic.

Up (also known has "Happy") endings are when the Hero wins and everything ends up well and good. These are the most popular endings, and thus are the most used. *Star Wars: A New Hope* has the perfect happy ending.

Down (also known as "Sad") endings are when the Hero loses and the Villain wins. But the Premise is still validated. It just means it's validated at the Hero's expense. These endings are rare nowadays. But in the deconstructionist 70s, you saw them a lot in movies. They are also common in horror films. *Butch Cassidy and the Sundance Kid* has a good example of the down ending. The Villain in this movie was authority. Authority (the law) won.

Ironic endings are where both the Hero and the Villain win and lose, thus canceling each other out. Examples of this are movies where the hero is a thief, he steals the million dollars, but as he escapes from the law, the money bag gets blown open and all the dollars fly off in the wind. *The Treasure of The Sierra Madre* has one of the best ironic endings ever written. So does *The Killing* and the original

The Italian Job.

It's possible to not end a story. There have been stories that just stop as if they ran out of pages or something. These endings are very unsatisfying and are not recommended. The creators of these stories often do that to show that life continues on. It doesn't just neatly wrap up like it does in fiction. The problem is, as we discussed, people want stories to make sense and have meaning. Stories are almost a substitute for religion. They create meaning out of meaninglessness.

Choose your ending wisely. Because it will be the last thing the Audience experiences before they leave the story. All stories don't need a happy ending. Negative endings are good for some stories. If you need to make a powerful statement, they are often the best endings to use. Ironic endings are great because most people see life as Ironic. They see the glass as both half full *and* half empty. People relate to seeing things evening out, because in most people's lives, they don't win the big game, but they don't lose it either. They just plod along with some high and low points in between.

The emotional highs a successful happy ending create is something most people want from a story, only because many of us use fiction to feel good.

This is why classic story structure is important to understand. If you want to be a successful writer, you must learn how to give people a pleasant buzz.

REMEMBER: Endings leave the reader with their last feeling and thought.

CHARACTERIZATION

"What is character but the determination of incident?
What is incident but the illustration of character?"
Henry James

WHAT IS CHARACTERIZATION?

This may surprise you, but characters are superior to real people. The reason is, characters are *clearer*. They're works of art.

Because they are knowable, you can understand characters better than real people. Real people are confused messes. We alternate our personas due to a mishmash of upbringing, attitude, world view, and neuro-chemical fluctuations. You may think you know someone really well and then they'll turn around and completely destroy your expectations in a second. Often in ways you would rather not discover. The truth about people is, we have sides we often keep hidden from the world and it takes certain things to reveal them.

This is why characters are much more appealing than real people. You can rely on them to be who they're supposed to be. And if they aren't you know it's the writer's fault.

If only people were that solid.

But to make good characters you need to understand the principles that make people what they are. Your goal isn't to imitate life. It's to *refine* it. To improve on it. A character is a distillation of human traits. You can either distill 100 proof hard liquor that blows the brain cells out the back of your skull, or you distill some watery crap no one will want to swallow. It's up to you.

Characters in a story are not independent of the plot just as we are not independent of reality. We can't just snap our fingers and stop time, or decide that the sky will be green today, or decide that we don't like the existing government so everything changes the second we feel it should be different. We all have to deal with reality as it comes to us and so do characters in a fictional reality.

This does not mean that characters in a story should just go with the flow. People have the power to change the course of events, and your hero in particular must affect change in some way. Otherwise there's no point in doing the story. If everything would proceed the same way without your hero's involvement, he's redundant.

The same holds true for the Villain. If the Villain has no impact on the events of the story, he isn't a real antagonist. He is unimportant and thus, disposable.

As we discussed earlier, conflict is the crux of every story. And conflict is transformed by dynamic will of the characters. When the will of the hero is pitted against the will of the villain it serves three purposes.

1. The conflict heats up and makes the story more exciting.

2. The character's are more thoroughly defined by their choices.

3. The premise is tested via its conflict with the counter premise.

But there is much more to characterization than the mere actions of the players. In order to make a character believable, you have to understand the principles of character dimension.

Character Dimensions

You've heard the term "two dimensional character", which is often used to describe a person without any depth, or a clichéd character in a story. None of us want our characters to come off as two dimensional, so there are certain criteria we need to understand. Let's explore the meaning of the term "character dimension."

A one dimensional character is a single minded individual with one noticeable personality trait. A hero, who is good. A villain, who is evil. Their personality is the same in any given situation. They just want to do what they were created for. That's their only purpose in life. You could call them plot robots. This what you see in cartoon characters. No depth. They are what they appear to be.

Two dimensional characters have one contradiction that makes them more complex than the one dimensional character. They are heroic, but are afraid of the dark. They are evil, but have some guilt. There isn't much more to them than that. But they have the illusion of depth because of their additional side. You might see that kind of character in told TV shows or mediocre movies.

Three dimensional characters, or more appropriately, *believable* characters have many contradictions. Simple examples are: A dictator out to conquer the world, who cares deeply about the preservation of his culture, but seeks to destroy others. He's a vegetarian, an artist, but has books burned he doesn't approve of. He's heavily for the advancement of science, but dabbles in mysticism and the occult. (There was a real person like that. His name was Adolf Hitler). Or how about a housewife who is a good mother, but cheats on her husband, is a secretly gay, likes bondage, and practices Buddhism.

But it takes more than a list of contradictions and characteristics to make a realistic character. The character's choices need to reflect their personal world view, their usual behavior and beliefs. There's also the matter of relational characterization which we'll discuss shortly. When writing three dimensional characters, choose your actions carefully at first. Once you get to know them, they will write themselves.

It's important to understand that every character in a story can't be three dimensional. Some character's roles are incidental, and making them too memorable could steal thunder from your main characters. So these walk on characters should be two dimensional in a non-cartoonish way. Unless you are going for a cartoon quality in your work.

The Power of Choice

Imagine a restaurant full of people. A gunman bursts in and starts shooting. Most will dive under the tables or hit the floor. Some will just cower there until they are killed. Some will try to escape. Some may even try to fight the gunman. Some will scream to God. Some will lose control of their bladders. Some will laugh hysterically. Some will cry uncontrollably. There are all kinds of possible reactions to this situation. What your character does, or chooses to do defines what your character is like at *that* moment in the story.

We are all defined by the choices we make in life. People form impressions based on how they see other people act, dress, and live. You choose what kind of clothes to wear. You choose your hair style. You choose to either be fit or fat. You choose to be lazy or industrious. You choose to be friendly or obnoxious. You choose to be honest or lie to yourself and others. You choose to be good or bad. This defines your character.

Many people act a certain way because of programming they've done to themselves over the course of their life, which was influenced by their environment, culture, family, friends and experiences. So much of their behavior is instinctive, rather than conscious. Even so, it is a clue to who they are and where their head is at. At some point, we chose to make ourselves the way we are.

People may choose to be lazy or mean, unconsciously, but it's still a powerful indicator of their psyche. Because it's saying they don't care enough to change. Or they lack the will. Or they are unable to see themselves in an objective light. And this can be very instructive and useful in a scene.

When you construct a character, you need to take these things into consideration. But to make your job easy, remember to think of the choices your character would make in the course of the story. Choices in clothes, choices in appropriate behavior, choices in verbal and emotional response.

Many writers mistakenly write their characters from the hip, basing the character's choices on their own idea of how to act. Or on clichés that this character is "supposed" to be like. This leads to one dimensional characters, and thus, to unmemorable fiction.

It's important to think about the character's choices when you have him respond to another character's action or dialog. When you have him walk into the room and announce themselves. When you have him choose something to eat in a restaurant.

But more importantly, there will be times where they will have to make *critical choices* that will have a major impact on the story. It will become very important to understand the nature of these critical choices. We will discuss this later.

REMEMBER: Choice is one of the most powerful tools of characterization.

THE RULES OF CHOICE

Choice behaves by certain rules. If you ignore these rules, you run the risk of offending your audience. Characters must be give logical choices which are not absolute. In other words, choices like: "Eat a bowl of ice cream or shoot your mother!" are not choices anyone is going to take seriously. Obviously, you would eat the bowl of ice cream. If you hated your mom that much you would have killed her by now.

A choice between right and wrong, good and evil isn't a worthwhile decision in fiction terms. If a hero makes an obviously wrong choice, the audience will lose their empathy for them and that is fatal to your story.

Therefore you need to create a third choice. And each choice should have attendant risks and benefits attached. They should be hard to choose between.

Example: Let's say you are forced to do a favor for a mobster or your best friend will be killed. The Choices are:

A: Take an unmarked package on board a plane.

B. Steal secrets from your employer that will help the mobster rob him.

C: Refuse.

Choice A seems like the safest choice, but the risks are obvious. Packages are scanned by detectors before being allowed on planes, dogs are used to sniff them for drugs. You may be arrested if it's contraband. And if you aren't arrested, you're still probably smuggling something bad. Then again, it could be innocent contents. This choice is morally ambiguous.

Choice B seems like a bad choice because it means stealing, and helping the mobster get more powerful. But it would also keep your friend alive. It also has less risks

121

attached. But it's also morally inferior to the first choice. This one seems immoral.

Choice C: The morally correct thing to do, but it would mean your friend's death and maybe your own. The audience would hate you, because no one likes a morally inflexible person. But you may want to say you refuse first, just to see if the mobster really means what he says. Then you could change your mind. Maybe.

You need to create choices with inherent risks, but they should also have benefits attached, otherwise, there is no motivation to do them. The benefit of A and B is that they will buy some time for your friend's. The benefit of C is you remain a morally correct person. Choosing A or B is more selfless and heroic. Choosing C would make you look like a person who cares about your morals more than other people's lives. It's not an empathetic position to take.

Most people would choose A as the most intelligent (unless they hated their boss, then they might gleefully choose B). Your audience will be choosing alongside your hero and hoping he makes their choice. This will increase their empathy for your character. They will find your character smart if he chooses what they thought was the right answer. But you then have to show them what the risk was in taking it. It can't just be that easy.

For choice A, let's call the hero Bob. Bob goes to the airport with the package the gangster handed him, sweating blood as he passes through security. Every cop seems to look at him with distrust. As the package goes through the X-ray scanner, Bob watches as the cops look at the video screen, then stop the conveyor belt so they can examine something that catches their eye. They turn to look at Bob, coldly. Or so he thinks. Bob frets, but tries to hide it. Suddenly, they let the package go on through. As

Bob walks to the plane, some DEA agents are coming toward him with a big dog on a leash. The dog looks at Bob and starts to make noises. But the DEA men don't notice. They're too busy talking about last night's football game. Bob hero gets on the plane, fastens his seat belt and lets out a sigh of relief. He made it. The package must be okay.

But, as the plane gets ready for take off, Bob notices a man two seats up on the left. He's a bitter rival of the gangster who made Bob take the package. Suddenly, he realizes the package could be a bomb! The gangster sent him on a suicide mission to kill an enemy. Oh, no! The plane starts to take off. It's too late to leave. Now what?

This is how you keep the story moving. Choice opens doors and allows your audience to participate in the story with the main character. But you don't stop with one choice being made. You create problems that force the character to make other choices as a result of their first choice.

If you do one of those stories where a character has to choose between three doors, one of which means freedom and the other two mean certain death. You're giving the audience a blind choice, where anything can happen. This tends to be unsatisfying because it feels random. This is why writers usually leave clues as to which door is the correct one, so the Hero can make an informed choice. It's not just a blind decision.

As we discussed earlier, people like a sense of order in their stories. They don't like randomness unless it's shown to have been part of a causal chain later in the story. For now, remember that characters must be given hard choices. Not obvious ones. And every choice *must* have repercussions.

If there are no stakes involved, the audience has no

reason to get excited. No reason to care. This is why gambling is so popular. Every game involves making choices, each with risks and potential pay offs. People love the excitement and the promise choices can offer them.

Emotional Choices

When we're feeling emotional about something we may behave out of character for the moment. A normally thoughtful person might make snap judgments when they're angry. A reckless person may be cautious when they're scared. It's important to think about the emotion of the character in a scene before you decide what they choose to do.

Remember the rules of choice, but also remember that audiences respond to emotions very strongly. Emotion has more resonance than logic. Logic is cold. Logic is somewhat impersonal. Emotion is very personal.

But you can't expect emotional empathy from the audience unless you've led them to feel that way first. Showing a person crying doesn't make the audience cry unless we've first been made to empathize with their struggle and pain.

You have to do that carefully, building up to those moments where you have emotional payoffs. An audience will understand a stupid choice if the character was in an emotional frame of mind where they'd be reckless. But you have to first convince the audience that this emotional state was arrived at realistically. People who suddenly change emotions at the drop of the hat are usually nuts. The term "Wacko" is applied to such people. Wackos don't create empathy in an audience. We can laugh at them, or disapprove of them, but don't expect too much sympathy.

REMEMBER: Make sure your characters have reasons

to be emotional when they make emotional choices.

RELATIONAL CHARACTERIZATION

Aside from the choices a character makes, and their contradictions, we have a third technique for defining them. I call it Relational Characterization.

Characters are also defined by the people they associate with. Who they choose as friends and lovers, who they make their enemies, can tell you a lot about a person. But more importantly, the *manner* in which people inter-relate defines their relationships with each other and reveals some of their sides.

We all react to different people in a different way. Some people turn us on. Some annoy us. Some make us mad. Some make us crazy. Some make us laugh. But not all the time. You may love your mom, but she may also drive you nuts. You may hate your boss, but you had a great time with him at the company picnic. There is a standard mode we have when dealing with certain people and there are other modes depending on our mood, the nature of the conversation, and the situation.

When you ask a friend for a loan, you probably use a different manner than when you're talking to him about a movie or asking him what you want to do for the evening. When using relational characterization it's important to stay aware of the context.

This is something we learn as children. We learn how to use different voices to get responses from our parents. We try different things to see what works, We continue this into adulthood. We use a different voice or inflection on people depending on the situation. We might put on our sexy voice for our lover, a high-pitched cutesy voice for our pet or children. We may use a tense, guarded voice for people we don't trust. And this defines not only our relationships with those people, but the way we feel about them.

The way certain people effect us can create impulsive emotional responses that we later regret. If someone hurt our feelings in the past, something may remind us of that in a conversation and all of a sudden we start saying mean things. These kind of responses are useful to be aware of. Such reactions can clue the Audience to important backstory elements that are revealed later.

Like I said, choice is a powerful indicator. In most cases we choose who we love and hate. And the reasons for this can speak volumes.

When you have a character talk to another character, you really need to understand the relationship they have and how it can reveal to the Audience sides of that character we don't usually get to see. It helps make that character seem more real and rounded out.

REMEMBER: A character is defined by their contradictions, choices, and relationships.

Symbolic Characterization

In addition to the above, there's a little technique you can use called Symbolic Characterization. This is mainly reserved for supporting characters. But it can be used for the Hero or the Villain, if done carefully.

Symbolic characterization is used when characters appearance and lifestyles are metaphors to enhance the premise, to set mood, or establish a theme. This is usually done through the use of archetypes in archetypal settings.

Comics love to use symbolic characterization because it's a medium of extremes. It started out showing people as exaggerated caricatures and it never quite lost that tendency.

Batman is a symbolic character. He dresses like a bat, lives (for all intents and purposes) in a cave, and only comes out at night. The Human Torch is a hot headed young man who turns into a living firebrand. Shakespeare made Richard III a ugly hunchbacked character, despite the fact that he was nothing of the kind in real life. He's visually symbolic of his persona.

But, it's dangerous to do this sort of thing without first making sure your character is well rounded. Otherwise they can become cartoony and unbelievable.

This hasn't stopped a lot of comic book writers from creating characters who looked like their personas. They are exactly what the seem. If you do this, don't expect too many readers to be impressed. It's been done to death.

You can also use symbolic characterization in contrast to the premise. Or to enhance some theme you're playing with in the story. There are a lot of ways to use it beyond the obvious.

REMEMBER: Characters need to be believable, even if they look strange.

THE HERO

Also known as the Protagonist. The hero is the center of good in the story. He is the person you root for. The Hero doesn't need to be good in the purest sense. In fact, people nowadays relate better to characters like themselves, flawed people trying to do the right thing, but not always succeeding. People who *try* to do good.

The key word here is try. Most people have an idea what "good" is, but not everyone agrees on what that is. Most people think of themselves as basically good. Even the most sordid criminals don't see themselves as bad. Defining who the hero is in a story is based on one or more of the following factors:

1. The consensus of positive characters in the story ultimately take the side of your hero.

2. The hero is a constructive force in the story, whereas the villain is destructive.

3. The hero, as champion of the premise, is vindicated when the premise is proved.

A good example of how a hero can be a villain or visa-versa, depending on the premise, can be demonstrated in Romanian Folk Tales about Vlad the Impaler, also known as Count Dracula.

In Romania, Vlad is a folk hero, despite the fact he butchered thousands of people. In neighboring countries, he is a monster. Even though both Romanians and their neighbors tell the same stories, Vlad changes from hero to villain depending on where the tale is told.

One story relates how some visiting dignitaries from Turkey came to visit Vlad at his castle. They didn't take off their hats in his presence. When he asked them why, they said it was a custom in their country never to remove their hat except when sleeping. Vlad then ordered his soldiers to nail the men's hats to their heads so they would never be tempted to disobey their custom. To an outside that sounds horrible. But the truth is, Turkey had been forcing countries like Romania to give up some of their children to fight in its armies. Those children would never see their families again and were converted to Islam. This had been going on for some time so Vlad was showing he was not putting up with any of Turkey's nonsense.

In the Romanian, the story's premise is "Foreigners should respect the customs of the land they visit." The story is used to show how Vlad taught those damn Turks a thing or two about manners. How dare they be so rude to a Romanian lord! Whereas in neighboring countries, the premise is: "Romanian lords are a bunch of psychotic despots."

Take the O.J. Simpson trial as an example. During the trial, one section of the country felt he was an innocent black man unfairly persecuted for marrying a white woman, while another section saw him as a murdering bastard who was treated with kid gloves *because* he was a rich, famous black man and the city of L.A. was afraid of another riot.

The people who thought he was innocent considered all the evidence against Simpson to be planted and made up, whereas the people who felt he was guilty thought the system was stacked in his favor because the defense could say whatever they wanted and didn't have to prove it, whereas the prosecution had to go through strenuous evidence hearings before they could present their data.

This is why the story of Simpson dominated the media so strongly during the time of the trial. The conflict between the premise and counter-premise was extremely hot. Furthermore, you could choose your heroes and villains easily. The players looked bad or good depending on your side. OJ's attorney, Johnny Cochran was either a smart, honest lawyer out to save his friend from the cruel jaws of society, or he was a sleazy con man out to free a rich pal that he knew, in his heart-of-hearts, was guilty. DA Marcia Clark was either a sharp, determined, underpaid civil servant battling corrupt, rich, connected attorneys out to free their wealthy client, or she was a vicious, cold bitch of a prosecutor, out to put away Simpson at any cost, just to advance her career.

In reality, it's no so cut and dry. Cochran could truly be sincere and still be wrong. Clark could be a bitch and still be right. In a good court room drama, these characters would be fleshed out so you're never completely sure about them until the conclusion of the story. This way the counter premise is able to give the premise a tough battle, making the story strong.

In reality OJ outed himself a few years later and is still serving time in a Nevada prison. That could be how you'd end that story, or if you took the OJ defense line, you would end it earlier before he made a fool out of himself.

In fiction, you need to decide who the hero is and work from there. The hero must be the underdog in every story. If the hero isn't battling insurmountable odds, they don't have a real conflict and thus, we have no story worth telling.

When the hero has too easy a time winning the Grail, the story has no punch. It's flat and anti-climactic. Nobody is interested in reading a story where there are no stakes. And nobody is interested in a hero that doesn't do anything special. The conflict is what makes the hero interesting. The way the hero deals with it, and their ability to overcome the conflict, is critical. So you have to make the stakes high or the story and your hero is going to

131

be awfully boring.

Empathy, not Sympathy

The Hero *must* be empathetic to the audience, not sympathetic. We must feel for him as an equal, even if we disagree with him. Empathy makes you feel for someone in a way you can relate to. Empathy is something you feel for an equal. For someone you see parts of yourself in.

Sympathy is a more distant emotion. It's what you feel for someone you don't relate to, but feel sorry for. You don't really see him as an equal. You don't see yourself in that person, but you feel bad for them anyway. You may feel sympathy for a wino begging for change, but you don't feel empathy for him. Not unless you see him as a peer.

Empathy is created when we see the hero of a story as the center of good. We know that, of the characters in the story, he is the one who is trying to make things right. He is trying to create order out of chaos. If the story is constructed properly, the audience will root for him as he journeys on his quest.

People, by nature, want to find the good in others. You create empathy by revealing a character's positive sides. Even when you're dealing with anti-heroes.

Anti-hero stories work when we feel empathy for the main character, despite the fact that he's a rotten bastard. Your Hero doesn't have to be Joe Perfect. He can be a crook. But we must feel empathy for him or you've lost.

In *Goodfellas*, Henry Hill was an empathetic character because he was a decent family man, wasn't psychotic like his pals. Henry basically tried to do good as he saw it. When he did bad things, it was often shown to be a logical action in his sordid milieu. Even though we knew it wasn't morally correct. You knew that he felt bad when he did it. This made him human to us.

REMEMBER: Empathy, not sympathy!

Choosing the hero

In some stories, we don't know who the Hero is at first. Sometimes we're given multiple protagonists to root for. By the end, one of them is the survivor, or is proven to be the winner of the Grail.

This technique is often used when you need to kill a protagonist to make the point of the premise stronger. A good example is in the musical *South Pacific*. The story starts when a young navy lieutenant, Joe Cable, arrives on a south seas island during World War II. Cable's reporting for a secret mission. He needs to convince an expatriate Frenchman, named Emile De Becque, to help him sneak onto another island De Becque knows well. The island is held by the Japanese and Lt. Cable's mission is to spy on them. De Becque doesn't want to do help Cable. He's middle-aged, successful, and in love with a young American nurse named Nellie Forbush.

It seems clear right away that the Lt. Cable is the hero of the story. But we discover later he really isn't. The true hero is the Nellie Forbush. The Lieutenant only serves as a device to validate the premise of the story. The Villain is preventing the Nellie from marrying De Becque. The same villain prevents Lt. Cable from marrying an island girl he falls in love with. Because both De Becque and Cable are losing to the Villain, they decide to go off to do the mission against the Japanese. Cable gets killed. This event helps Nellie defeat the Villain and marry De Becque in the end. Who is the Villain? More on that later.

Every story can have multiple protagonists, but usually, there is only one character who is the real hero of the story. They are the Grail winner. They will be the one to walk away with the glory at the end. But that doesn't mean they have to survive. As we'll discuss later, there are three possible endings to a story. And you decide which one makes the point better. The hero can win the Grail in a whole lot of ways. Not just by victory.

REMEMBER: The hero is the champion of the premise, whether they like it or not.

THE VILLAIN

Also known as the Antagonist, the Villain is usually the champion of the counter premise. The Villain is often the center of evil in the story. It is from him that the conflict arises. He's usually behind the dilemmas facing the hero and he's in direct opposition to the hero obtaining the Grail. Because he stands in the way, he is usually a lot closer to the Grail than the Hero is.

Unlike the Hero, however, the villain doesn't have to be a person. It can be a force of nature, or merely something as abstract as life itself. The Villain can be the Hero's insecurities, it can be an addiction, it can be poverty, or an illness.

Remember our discussion of *South Pacific*? In that story the villain was bigotry. Nellie Forbush didn't want to marry Emile De Becque because he'd been married to a South Seas Islander and has two children of a mixed race. Nellie was from Arkansas and was raised by a bigoted mother, so it was hard for her to shake her upbringing. Lt. Cable didn't want to marry the island girl for similar reasons. He loved her, but he knew society back home would ostracize him and he didn't feel good about that. Later, when on his mission, Cable decides to stay on the island after the war and marry her anyway. But he gets killed before that can happen. His death shows Nellie how pointless bigotry is and how it stands in the way of love between all people. She overcomes the Villain of the story and marries De Becque.

South Pacific broke all Broadway records in its day. It was Rogers and Hammerstein's most successful work. But generally speaking, the audience prefers human villains in their stories. Or humanoid, if you will, since a lot of the villains in comic books and fantasy can't really be called human.

Villains don't have to be evil, or even bad. They can be well meaning individuals. After all, some of the worse crimes in history were caused by well meaning individuals. The Inquisition was supposed to weed out the sinners, the Missionaries tried to save people around the world by destroying their culture, the U.S. Government interned Japanese Americans during World War II to make our country safe. We know now that all these people were wrong, but at the time, they had "good" intentions.

Most "Villains" in real life think of themselves as the Hero. They think they are doing the right thing. If you're a liberal, you might see Rush Limbaugh as a villain. If you're a conservative, you might see Jon Stewart as a villain. And if you're a centrist, you might see them both as villains. A Villain is anyone who is not on "our" side. When you decide who the Hero of the story is, you're telling the audience which side to take. You then have to make the audience root for the Hero and boo the Villain. But the Villain does not have to be evil. He can even be sympathetic.

Most of the evil in our world is caused by stupidity or greed, not by willful destruction. When you create a Villain, it's more instructive to the Audience to see one that represents problems they can relate to. People generally don't relate to an alien who wants to rule the planet because they're evil. But give them a Villain who wants to steal from them or make their life miserable because it serves his own personal gain, and the Audience can relate to it in some way. Most of us have been victimized at some point or another by such people.

You also make a Villain more believable when you reveal their inner pain. Most criminals are doing ill because that's what they've been taught all their lives. Or they've been traumatized a long time ago and are acting out to dull the pain. Or they're trying to get some pay back for perceived injustices. Or they're trying to get ahead the fast way because their lives are terrible and they can't take the pain. They're addicted to the rush of trying to win through danger.

Your villain must have a strong reason for what he does. He can't just be doing it because he's evil. There must be something in it for him. The stakes for the villain should be just as high as they are for the hero. That way, the story becomes more exciting as it builds toward the climax. Failing that, you should at least create some reasons why the villain must succeed. As the champion of the counter premise, his side demands equal time.

The Villain should be as believable as your hero. Maybe more so. After all, the hero in a story is only as good as the Villain. The Villain creates the conflict. If you have a weak Villain, you have a weak conflict. Then your hero doesn't look heroic.

Villains are Superior!

The Villain should always have the upper hand until the climax of the story. If the Villain isn't winning, you lose the conflict. Say good-bye to the audience at that point. Ever notice how people start walking out of the theater before the credits roll, because they know the movie's ended? They don't call it the climax for nothing. Once people have their fun, they're outta there!

The Villain is the pull, the *driving force* behind the conflict. You need the Villain to be powerful. The Villain has to put the hero on the ropes. The Villain can never show weakness in the story until the climax. Otherwise, people will lose interest. Guaranteed.

The Villain must be superior to the hero in some way.

In *South Pacific*, the Villain was a powerful psychological force that prevented the heroine from truly opening her heart to the one she loved. The Villain was winning up until the end. In *Terminator 2*, the T-1000 was an unstoppable force right up to the last scene. In Jaws, the shark was relentlessly kicking Roy Schieder's scrawny butt until he got lucky.

Nobody cares if your hero can beat up a weakling. That isn't heroic. The Villain has to be superior in a way that matters. If not brawn, then brains. If not brains, then skill. But the Villain *must* be superior.

REMEMBER: Weak Villain, weak story.

SUPPORTING CHARACTERS

These fall into Four basic categories: Protagonists, Antagonists, The Chorus, Extras.

They're called supporting characters because they exist in the service of the Hero. It's that simple. The Hero is the sun around which all other characters orbit in some way. This is why some literary theorists describe the Hero as the pivotal character.

Supporting characters give your Hero and Villain something to work with. They help define your main characters and advance the plot. They define your characters by revealing their sides, as we discussed in relational characterization.

If a character serves no purpose in a story, they shouldn't be there. You don't want unnecessary distractions. You don't have the luxury of that, especially in comics where the amount of space available is always limited. So choose your characters wisely and get the most value out of them.

We don't have all the facts at our disposal in life. Neither do your Heroes or Villains. The supporting characters exist to supply the Hero or Villain with information, advance the story, and/or support the premise in some way. Here's a definition of the types.

Protagonists: These are the sub-heroes of the story. Like the Hero, they're fighting for the premise. They are against the Villain. They either help the hero on his quest or are fighting along side of him for the similar reasons. They may be friendly competitors, even. We root for the Protagonists. Sometimes we may be tricked into thinking they are the Hero, as we did in South Pacific, so we're surprised when they die. Basically, they exist to help the hero in some way by providing information or the lucky breaks he needs to succeed. They can also be the love interest. In super-hero team comics, the other members in the team are the protagonists. The Hero is the one character around which that particular story revolves.

Antagonists: They are the Villain's accomplices, his minions. Sometimes, like the Protagonists, they work on the side of the Villain, but not with him. They may be friendly competitors or they may be helping him without their knowledge. Like the Villain, they don't have to be a real person, they can be a concept or a force of nature. Whatever they are, they add to the conflict. They are in opposition to the hero.

The Chorus: In Greek Plays these characters served to provide commentary on the action in the story. For our purposes, the Chorus is any character who exists to provide information in the story. Examples of a Chorus character include: The scientist who provides the Hero with technical information he needs, the street informant the Hero shakes down for leads, the store clerk who tells him where the phone is, etc.

Extras: These characters are basically window dressing. They help enhance the mood or feel of a scene. Examples include the filthy bum panhandling for change, the waiter at a restaurant, the sexy girl who flirts with the Hero, the angry mob.

For all intents and purposes, the supporting characters are devices to advance the story. But they should *never* seem to be anything less than real people. It should *never* be obvious to the Audience that these characters are just there to serve the plot. To avoid this you should create strong motives for them being where they are and knowing what they know. Believability is critical.

It's possible to put supporting characters in orbit

around each other to help define them. Since each character pulls on a different aspect of another, this is a sound way to define their dimensions.

The same rules of characterization apply to supporting characters, but you don't want to make extras complex unless they come back in another story. Extras are there as eye candy or to create mood and polarity. You want to focus on the hero and the villain in your story and only expand on the other characters as relevant to your tale.

So try to bring life to the supporting cast without going overboard.

If you're writing an adventure story it's not a good idea to let the supporting characters steal thunder from your hero. You don't want them to make your hero look bad, or too dependent on them. You want them to only support him as they're needed. If the Hero needs their advice or counsel too much, he looks weak. Furthermore, if they think too much for him, figure out too many things for him, the Hero looks dumb. So be careful.

REMEMBER: Every character must have a purpose. Supporting characters support.

ARCHETYPES

You may have noticed that human personalities seem to fall into categories. Some people are clownish, some are mean, some are serious, some are childish, some are bland. There are several basic human models that everyone recognizes. These are called Archetypes. From these models you can extrapolate a personality and build on it, since no one is 100% archetypal. Men and woman can be a combination of any of these archetypes. But people tend to want to be a certain way, so that's the face they present to the world. The Archetype tells us what their mask is.

Like many things we take for granted today, the concept of the archetype has its origins in ancient Greece. The root words are *archein*, which means "original or old"; and *typos*, which means "pattern, model or type". The combined meaning is an "original pattern" of which all other similar persons, objects, or concepts are derived, copied, modeled, or emulated. Most, if not all, people have several archetypes at play in their personality construct; however, one archetype tends to dominate the personality in general. It can be helpful to know which archetypes are at play in oneself and others, especially loved ones, friends and co-workers, in order to gain personal insight into behaviors and motivations. It will help you to craft believable characters.

In modern times, the psychologist, Carl Gustav Jung, used the concept of archetype in his theory of the human psyche. He believed that universal, mythic characters—archetypes—reside within the collective unconscious of people the world over. As Jung saw it, archetypes represent fundamental human motifs of our experience as we evolved; consequentially, they evoke

142

deep emotions.

Jung defined twelve primary types that symbolize basic human motivations. Each type has its own set of values, meanings and personality traits. Also, the twelve types are divided into three sets of four, namely Ego, Soul and Self. The types in each set share a common driving source, for example types within the Ego set are driven to fulfill ego-defined agendas.

Let's first examine the twelve before we explore some others.

The Ego Types

The Innocent: This is a familiar character in a lot of stories, especially fantasies like Lord of the Rings and the Hobbit. A protagonist who is basically a good person who wants to lead a peaceful life and has no loft ambitions other than that. They become a template upon which a more complex character gets built through trials.

The Everyman: Similar to the innocent but often carrying around some kind of secret pain or loss. The everyman is down to earth, a solid citizen. They operate on common sense and represent the average soul. They are also a starting point but not necessarily going to change other than to learn new things.

The Hero: Unlike the Everyman, the Hero is a leader or the focus of attention. The hero stands out from a crowd. The Hero is often created from the template of the first two by going through trials. The Hero can know fear but they overcome it. The hero is not afraid of conflict. The hero overcomes or dies trying.

The Caregiver: While the Hero acts to defeat things like people, monsters and situations, the Caregiver is a healer. They're a helper and a companion who soothes and provides solace of some kind. They might be a mother or a priest. They are often a conscience character who acts as a sounding board. They are a protector and in many cases a provider of things,

The Soul Types

The Explorer: The explorer is someone who is always searching for something new. Who is always wanting to know what's over the next hill. The explorer is represented by someone like Indiana Jones. They might be heroic but their motivation is a desire to find something or uncover some truth.

The Rebel: This is a person either angry or extremely dissatisfied with the status quo. And they want to fight the system, tear it down even. They are radical in either their politics or their position on a subject of theirs'. They tend to be outlaws and troublemakers. They also tend to be hard to get along with.

The Lover: The lover is a soul mate or a very positive force in the life of another. The lover is caring, sharing, nurturing. They are a different aspect of the caregiver.

The Creator: Also known as the Artist. The creator is a person who is driven by the art that they chose. They seek mastery if it, They strive to be original. They may be a painter, a musician, an actor or a writer. No matter what form their creativity takes, it is a driving force in their personal life. Many times a creator is working through personal pain by using their art as therapy. The creator is a more down to earth version of the Magician.

The Self Types

The Jester: A clown, a joker, the jester rarely takes things seriously. The is an escapist, trying to always have a good time. Usually because he doesn't want to deal with life or secret pain he has. The Jester is mercurial and often unpredictable. Also known as the trickster. They often delight on making others uncomfortable. Because they are never comfortable themselves.

The Magician: The magician is similar to the creator except they are about transforming reality in some way. Changing one state into another. Always trying to accomplish the impossible. Often trying to make a miracle happen. They firmly believe in miracles. The magician can be a shaman, a inventor, a healer. Tony Stark of Iron Man fits this archetype.

The Sage: Also known as the Philosopher. The sage is a seeker of truth. They wish to use intelligence and analysis to understand the world. They are often teachers, mentors, experts, detectives, scholars.

The Ruler: The ruler is a leader so believes power is an ultimate goal. They may be seeking power through wealth or influence or politics but they wish to command other people's fortunes and control destiny. Their secret pain may be that they come from nothing and never want to return there. They are driven and focused and never rest. They are constantly onto the next goal.

— — — — — — — — — — — -

Now, here are more archetypes from fiction.

The Hero: Athletic, confident, handsome, successful, a leader. A model of what everyone wants to be, but most people are jealous of.

The Saint: Pure, noble, kind, humble, understanding. Usually a religious figure.

The Nice Guy: Kind, thoughtful, helpful, sympathetic, sweet, unthreatening, easy going, dependable, a real pal.

The Harlot: Earthy, flirtatious, wanton, wild, instant mood swings, want's fun all the time, easily bored, non-committal, freewheeling, looking for a free ride.

The Drunk: Can't deal with reality, looking for escape, wants to get high, stoned, drunk, laid, anything to take their mind off the pain they're carrying around inside. Sticks to light conversation, irresponsible, self destructive. Usually insecure.

The Cheerleader: Bouncy, cheerful, positive, grinning, happy, cooperative, an organizer, a shill, a back patter, often touchy-feely, wants to be your friend, is always UP!

The Sensitive: Wants to get involved with causes, self righteous, judgmental, ideological, cynical, passionate, tends to demonize opponents, is prone to zealotry, can be demagogic and polemical, considers themselves torch carriers for "values", thinks they feel empathy but are really only capable of sympathy.

The Egotist: Usually intelligent, but over bearing, self absorbed, self centered, insensitive to other people's feelings, a know it all, a braggart, talks about themselves a lot, free with their opinions, but doesn't have much interest in anyone else's, thinks he deserves everything he wants, basically a spoiled brat.

The Dreamer: Intelligent, lots of aspirations, low drive, daydreams a lot, generally inactive, easy going, usually set in their ways, capable of doubt, but addicted to denial and rationalization, always expects to win the lottery, good hearted but frivolous, generally a nice person but is often irresponsible.

The Drone: Bland, responsible, doesn't rock the boat, keeps head down, plays the game, low confidence, slow about everything they do, waiting for retirement. Dependable.]

The Masochist: No self esteem, a weakling and a coward, thinks he's bad, feels guilty about everything, feels he deserves to be treated bad even though he doesn't really want it, often keeps these feelings to himself, but radiates the above vibes even so. Often gives off strange sexual vibes, like they're a voyeur in need of a show.

The Dejected: Depressed, weepy, miserable, gloomy, unhappy, or all of the above. A half empty type person. Never satisfied, nothing pleases, always looking for the fault in things, distrustful of any altruistic gesture, always looks on the dark side.

The Boss: A workaholic, driven, a bottom liner, cuts to the chase, no time for protocol, wants it yesterday, doesn't care about your feelings or problems, demanding, serious, cheap.

The Grouch: Brooding, angry, paranoid, distrustful, a loner, a shut in. Usually a mean old man.

The Shark: Opportunistic, selfish, conniving, manipulative, heartless, charming when necessarily, cold the rest of the time, greedy, ambitious, driven, always HUNGRY for more.

The Villain (also known as The Sadist): Spiteful, vicious, sadistic, power mad, egotistical, cruel, greedy, out for blood, plays games, sick sense of humor.

Everyone has met a version of these archetypes, so they have powerful resonance in a story. That is why you see these characters in fiction all the time. But no one is a pure archetype. Usually, qualities of the others are mixed in.

Some archetypes are actually masks that people have chosen as their persona. The Jester and The Cheerleader are usually fronts for deep pain or insecurity. The same rule applies to the Grouch. The Grouch is often a good person inside, who is afraid of being hurt by other people, so they take the persona as a defense. The Cheerleader is often the Shark or the Grouch in disguise. The Clown is often the Grouch or the Egotist in reality. The Saint is often the Boss or the Shark. The Hero is often a great looking, lucky version of the Boss or the Drone.

REMEMBER: Archetypes are a base to work from but not the whole person.

PERSONALITY

Personality comes in three basic flavors: Boring, interesting, and scary. You need to determine which version of the latter two you want your characters to have, because boring is the last thing you want a character to be.

Of course, there are times you will want a boring character for the sake of contrast, or to make some kind of point. But even then, you have to make them interesting enough to keep our attention.

Think of a small party of people. Notice how some people seem to always stand out of a crowd. They seem to get all the attention. As a writer, you've got to figure out what they're doing right that makes them interesting to others and use that to your advantage.

Of course, popular people are usually very shallow and superficial to talk to. This is because they're afraid of their own inner demons and they are on the run from their own neuroses. They don't want to get into any conversations that might expose this or dredge up thoughts they're trying to avoid. Your characters can be like that if you want, but they still have to be empathetic.

Popular individuals are favored because they retain mystery about themselves. They stay away from positions that are unsafe. They don't reveal their inner pain or their personal problems. At the same time, they uplift the mood of a scene. The "life of the party" is always someone with a sense of humor, a schmoozer who knows how to please. Depressed or angry individuals are a turn off, even if they are mysterious.

Another way people achieve popularity is by stroking another's ego in a non-obsequious way. They do it by treating the other person as a peer, rather than a superior. But doing it too much is obvious and it comes off insincere. You have to find the right balance.

So creating a personality that is positive and somewhat mysterious should be your main goal. Your hero cannot look like a wimp internally, even if they do externally. You can peel away the layers of mystery as the story unfolds. But never tell us too much about a person right off the bat.

It's one of the first things a person learns about dating. Never tell the other person everything about yourself. It will inevitably bore them or put them off. The less someone knows, the more they need to find out. That gives them something to work for. It's like a carrot on a stick. We need motivations in life. Nothing has value unless we struggle for it. So relationships that have the most appeal are always the those involving a chase. We chase after what we think we see and want. The less we know about someone, the more we can project our fantasies and ideals on them.

The great psychologist Carl Jung proposed a theory that we project our inner most desires on people we are attracted to. We make them what we want them to be in our minds. They are never truly what we believe them to be. And if we see that demonstrated in some way it's very disappointing and hurtful. Character personas are idealized human personalities. We create clear individuals we can understand. So it's necessary to reveal what we want the reader to know at that point in time, so they will form this idealized model of the character in their minds while reading.

A character's personality needs to grab our attention. They have to light up every scene. Naturally, the Hero is the main bonfire. We don't want the supporting cast to get to steal the show, though it can happen. Make sure the Hero and Villain keeps us spellbound. Their personality needs to outshine the other characters in the story.

Scary personalities are the kind crazy people have. They make us worried that it could rub off. Or they remind us of that old adage: "There, but for the grace of God, go I." Scary characters are great for spiking the energy of a scene. The Frank Booth character in *Blue Velvet* really grabbed our attention every time he was on camera. But you have to be careful with these kind of characters because they can lapse into parody very easily.

Components of a Persona

The human persona can be broken down into three main components. Intellectual, Emotional, and Habitual. Some people are more prone to reason than emotion. Some are the opposite. And many people have unconscious habits which are displayed randomly or most of the time. These habits can indicate certain neuroses or psychological traits that can be used for characterization purposes. When constructing a character's persona it's not a bad idea to keep these three things in mind and see how they can be used to your advantage.

Personas, Masks and Facades

It's important to understand that for many people, their personality is something they constructed as a tool for interacting with society. It's not who they really are. It's a mask. The real person is far more complex. If you could read people's minds, you'd see their true persona hiding behind the facade.

We all know that how people act under normal circumstances is misleading. We can never be sure of a person's true intentions, even if we know them well. There's only one way to really get to see the inside of someone's head and that's when they are put under pressure. The cowards run and the heroes let the fists fly when it all hits the fan. When the Audience knows where a character really stands on an issue, they can be more comfortable with them.

In life, this is how you find out who your real friends are. When they are tested by the cruel twists of fate. The term "Fair Weather Friend" is known to us all. We've seen who sticks by our side when things get rough and who doesn't return our calls.

In a story, you need to put a lot of pressure on your characters. They need to be tested, put through the fire. We need to see what kind of person they really are, what they are truly made of. And that's what the Audiences want to see.

Pressure

Pressure can come in many forms. Through relational characterization, we can show how a normally cool character becomes flustered when his mother is around. By using choice as a tool, we can present the character with problems where the solution they choose determines their moral backbone. We can also cause the character a world of hurt to see how they react to it. The Villain can force them to do something against their will, and we can see how they deal with it.

Pressure is another critical force in storytelling. No pressure, no conflict, no story.

No one cares about people who have an easy time. We might get jealous, but we won't be impressed. You want your hero to impress us.

There are exceptions, of course. James Bond seems to have an easy time doing certain things. But if you watch the movies, you'll notice the best ones are the stories where he was under the most pressure to succeed. Ultimately, James Bond's ability at cards or seducing women isn't the skills that matter. It's not how he overcomes the Villain. He does that using his wits and his brawn and usually, they are put to the test.

The job of a plot is to put pressure on the characters so we can see who they are and what they're made of. Until that happens, your hero is just another citizen.

REMEMBER: True character is revealed under pressure.

CHARACTER CONSTRUCTION

Now that we've discussed some of the fundamentals of characterization let's explore the construction of a character. First off, we need to decide what role the character takes in the story. Are they Hero, Villain, Protagonist, Antagonist, or Chorus? Determine how much we need to know about them for the purposes of the story, then answer the following questions. These are questions you must know the answers to. Utterly. If you're building a supporting character who just has a minor role, it's still not a bad idea to know as much as possible about them. You may want to expand their role later. Or it may give you insights that could be useful when writing their dialog.

Name
Gender
Age
Height, Weight
Color of Hair, Eyes, Skin
Appearance: Attractive, average, ugly, clean, dirty, athletic, flabby, etc.
Archetypal models
Alignment: Saintly, good, troubled, bad, evil
Race
Class: Aboriginal, Homeless, Lower, Middle, Upper
Occupation, income
Work hours, work ethic
Education
Home life: Married, single, children, lives with parents
Religion
Nationality or Culture
Place in Community: Clubs, sports, lodges, etc.

Amusements: Hobbies, Interests, Pastimes

Politics: Conservative, Liberal, Middle of the Road, Communist, Anarchist

Favorite foods

Sexual Orientation: Hetro, BI, Gay, Transsexual, Pedophile, etc.

Sex Life: Promiscuous, Virgin, Celibate, gets it when he can

Fetishes: Sexual, compulsive, objects that are always kept on him

Morality, Standards

Ambitions, Goals, Dreams

Attitude: Militant, relaxed, resigned, defeatist

Complexes: Obsessions, Inhibitions, superstitions, phobias, hang ups

Illusions (what false beliefs to they hold onto)

Abilities: Languages, Talents

Qualities: Imagination, intellect, judgment, taste, poise

I.Q.

Superpowers, if applicable

Once you've answered the main questions, as needed, we then proceed to the second series of important character building questions. Answer all that are pertinent with the story you're writing. Or if important to the backstory.

Relationships
1. Parents: Alive or dead?
2. Relationship with parents: Good, bad, indifferent, communicative, loving
3. Step parents, relations with
4. Siblings, Relations with siblings
5. Lovers, relations with

6. Ex-Lovers, relations with
7. Other Relations
8. Enemies
9. Employers
10. Who do they trust?
11. Who do they hate?
12. Who do they love?
13. Who do they desire?
14. Who do they fear?
15. Who do they loathe?
16. Who do they need?

For the Hero and Villain, you should know most or all by heart depending on the relevance to your story. The relational questions will help you choose the right characters to present when using relational characterization.

Character backstory

We can safely assume your characters weren't born yesterday. They had a life leading up to the first moment they appear in your story. The events that shaped their lives and their psyches is called backstory. It's the accumulation of their experiences from birth until the time of your tale.

You should know the backstory of all...and I do mean all...of your characters. You may not need to know every little detail, but you should have a clear idea. The above lists of questions are a good way to work it out. Get a notebook and answer every question. When you're done you'll feel you know the character a lot better. And when you write them they'll be more real in your mind. They may even "write themselves".

Backstory is also important when it involves the story you're doing. Something in this character's past may have an impact on the events in your plot. You should think through what those events are and also the time and place they occurred. Something that happened in the 1970s should be looked at from the perspective of that time. Not this time. Each decade has it's own feel and attitude and looking back on those times should feel appropriate to the audience.

People are also a product of the time and place they were raised in. Study people from the generation your character comes from for clues, if you aren't of that generation.

Those who were raised prior to the 1960s tend to have a whole different world view than those born later. Baby boomers tend to have a different outlooks, attitudes and expectations than "Generation Xers" do. It's important to take these things into account.

Although it's become a trite device in contemporary fiction, the hidden trauma in a character's past can also contribute to the persona of a character. But it should never be used as an excuse for why someone acts the way they do. A human persona can't be attributed to one event in the character's life. People are far more complex than that.

This hasn't stopped a lot of writers from falling into the trap of using pop psychology to explain away a character's entire personality based on something like Child Abuse or some other taboo of the week.

But there's no reason for you to follow in their footsteps, unless you like being lame.

REMEMBER: Backstory is relevant, but it shouldn't be used to rob a character of their mystery.

ALIGNMENT

The audience needs to understand more than what kind of persona a character has, or even their backstory. The thing they really want to know is whether the character is good, bad, or neutral.

Terms like good and bad are really meaningless unless you demonstrate what kind of good or bad. There are good people who are useless, there are bad people who are harmless. We need to know the level of good and the level of bad in a practical way. We do that by demonstrating their alignment in a manner that gauges their level. Examples of levels:

GOOD: Helpful, kind, sincere, trustworthy, heroic, generous, complimentary, uplifting

BAD: Cruel, deceitful, violent, lying, depressing, psychotic, a thief, a rapist, a murderer

Good characters provide information, materials, love, anything that helps the hero on his quest. Bad characters have the opposite effect. They take. They work against the hero's quest. It's possible for a character to alternate from bad to good in a story, but in the end they should come out on one side of the equation or the other.

Neutral doesn't mean the same thing here as it does in role playing games. It means neither positive or negative. This is something you don't really want any character to be in a story unless you are planning to use them in some surprising way. But even then, you want to demonstrate some aspect of their alignment before hand. A neutral character would be like a guy who is standing in the corner and never says anything or does anything.

Neutral characters can be used for the sake of irony, however. They could act as a lighting rod to cancel out the charge of a scene. This would be someone who does bad and good to the hero in equal measures, canceling out their impact on the scene. But this is a dangerous thing to play around with unless you're really sure of what you're doing.

As human beings, we like to know where we stand with the people around us. We like to know if that guy over there is safe or dangerous. The audience is going to want to know these things about every character in the story. You tell them what they want to know by demonstrating the character's alignment. But, the characters in the scene don't always have to be aware of it. Just the Audience.

These demonstrations will add to the power of the scene or panel, because they create more empathy or antipathy for the characters in question.

When creating your cast of characters, it's a good idea to create people who are polar opposites, or at odds in some way. This incites conflict which adds to the dramatic tension of your story. Choosing the alignments of the characters will help you decide how effective their presence will be to a scene.

The alignment of a character should be demonstrated in every scene they appear in. Naturally, many characters will not always play the same role. A helpful character can become harmful later. That's fine. Just make sure you display the nature of their alignment at the proper time.

REMEMBER: Alignment defines on which side characters stand.

STEREOTYPES

Needless to say, you should avoid stereotypes when creating characters. But the truth is, there are people who look and act like living clichés. All stereotypes got started somewhere, and certainly there are people who fit the bill.

But we need avoid clichéd characters for one simple reason.

It's been done.

Forget right or wrong. Your first goal as a writer is to be interesting. You can write objectionable fiction and still be entertaining as hell. Quentin Tarantino and Robert Crumb made a career out of it. You decide what is right when you set out to tell a story. Fiction is your statement. Your argument. Your goal is not to placate sectors of the public, because no matter what you do, someone will be offended anyway.

But you don't want to write characters with contempt. Every person is an individual with unique thoughts and feelings. Your goal as a writer is to create characters that are distinct personalities. A stereotype is nothing more than a cartoon. It doesn't do justice to its subject. It may be used for humorous effect, but it will never be taken seriously in drama. People are bored with clichés.

If you go to write a character from a different race or culture than your own, question the character choices you make. Try to create a real person *before* you settle on their ethnicity or culture. That way you can avoid creating a stereotype.

One of the most important tools you will need as a writer of characters is empathy. Your characters may be nothing but creations of your mind. But you should look at them as people and try to understand why they are the way they are. You should understand what their secret pain is or what drives them from a human perspective. People will understand them better and invest more in the narrative if they believe the characters.

REMEMBER: Stereotypes are clichés.

TECHNIQUE

"There are no dull subjects. There are only dull writers."

H.L. Mencken

TECHNIQUE

"The more subtle and elegant you are in hiding your plot points, the better you are as a writer."
Billy Wilder

We've just learned all basics of writing, from the definitions of story and plot to the basics of story structure. Now we're going to delve into the more advanced area of technique. These are the tools you'll use to make your story stronger. Knowing how to structure a story is only the beginning. Once you lay down the structure, you then have to fine tune it.

Technique should never be obvious. It should be invisible. The Audience should not be aware that it's there. The mark of a good writer is their ability to make the technique in their story disappear. They make the story look "easy". It seems compelling and real. Self aware writing that spends part of its time showing you how clever the writer is by beating you over the head with technique is bad writing. No matter how slick and intelligent such writing may seem, it's not good if it's beating you up with technique. Stories are meant to be enjoyed for what they are, not for how they are made.

There is an exception to this principle. Comedy or surrealistic structure allows you to break down the fourth wall and expose the writer's hand. But in stories that are meant to be taken seriously, the writer's hand should never be obvious. Distractions are a sin in fiction. You don't want the Audience to stop reading all of a sudden to notice some trick you are pulling. You don't want them to fall out of the trance a good story puts you in.

Your job is to seduce them, not to jump up and down and brag about yourself. You want them to get into the mood and into your bed. Self aware writing tends to spoil the mood. So it's not a good idea.

Now for the technique.

SET-UPS AND PAY OFFS

"If a shotgun hangs on the wall in the first act, it must be used by the climax." **Anton Chekov**

The great playwright Anton Chekov, who brought us "The Seagull". Chekov was right, even though he often broke his own rule.

Any item or skill that is critical to the story in some manner, must be set up in the story before you use it. When you use the item that is known as the "pay off". But it doesn't stop with items and talents. Lots of things need setting up before being used.

First let's understand the set up. It exists to tell the Audience that this item, talent, power, whatever, exists in the Milieu. This way, when it's used later in the story it doesn't seem random. We know that it can happen. As we discussed in an earlier chapter, the Audience expects reality to be reasonably emulated by your story. So things need to behave according to some rules. Objects don't appear out of the blue in reality, so they shouldn't in your story.

If a character ends up performing brain surgery later in the story and we were never told they were a doctor, the Audience loses their suspension of disbelief, and we know what that means. They're gone.

People don't like being lied to. They don't like being made to look like fools. If you surprise them in a nice way, they like it. But if you expect them to swallow an absurdity that's meant to be taken seriously, they'll become disgusted with you.

So first you have to let them know that something is coming. But you have to do it in a way that isn't spoiling the surprise your planning. A bad set up makes for a weak pay off.

Set ups are best done visually. When you set something up with dialog, it doesn't stick in the mind as well as when people see it. Expositional dialog is also a pain to write naturally. So why make it difficult for yourself? If your character needs to perform a medical operation later in the story, all you need to do is show a Doctor's Degree on their wall early in the story. Or show a business card that says he's a doctor. In prose your character in the scene will notice the object you want to be seen. And you can always make it a prop in some way, so it is handled to make it extra clear that it's there. Like, for example, someone picks up a book of matches on someone's table and notices it's from a bar with an usual name. That bar will show up later in the story, and the book of matches shows that the character who owns them was there before.

The same rule applies to super powers, martial arts skills, the ability to solve puzzles quickly, weapons that are used later, you name it. Anything that is crucial to the story must be set up before hand. And the sooner the better.

Since nothing in a story should go to waste, you shouldn't set up anything you don't plan to use. Unless you're trying to trick the audience into thinking the story is going in a different direction than it actually is. You may want to set up some weapon, for example, but when the character goes to use it later, he find out it doesn't work. This creates a powerful reversal which forces the hero to find another means to win the day.

When you don't want the audience to see something coming, you should get your set up in early. That way, they may forget about it until later when you finally do the pay off. The object of a set up is to tell the audience that these things are in the world of the story, so they don't just get pulled out of a hat later. People feel a story is bad when that happens. They may not understand why, but they instinctively feel the writer is bad. So make sure you set things up.

Pay offs are, in essence, the punch lines to the set up. A set up tells you a piece of information. But it's an incomplete piece. It's only the first half, like the first part of a joke. You don't get it until the punchline is thrown at you.

A pay off can be a tremendous boost if it turns out to be extremely important to the story and you set it up cleverly. Alfred Hitchcock movies are worth studying for his use of set ups and pay offs. In *Vertigo*, Jimmy Stewart's character has a fear of heights. During the Turning Point, this fear pays off because it prevents him from seeing a murder. His need to overcome this fear is what allows him to solve the riddle of the crime at the end. So the set up doubles as a bit of characterization which leads to the character's development. In *Sabotuer* the Hero accidentally bumps into a man who later turns out to be a villain. The man drops some letters. When the Hero picks them up he sees an address on them and the name of the sender. This information becomes vital to him later because he gets accused of being a saboteur. The set up was his link to find the Villain. Unfortunately, the information was misleading. So the pay off is also a reversal.

It's good to make each pay off count in more ways than one. If you can make them not only relevant to the story as information, but also a means of advancing the character or the conflict, you will get a much cooler scene for your effort. But more importantly, it helps create epiphanies for the audience.

Revelations

Have you ever ready a story where you were fed tiny little clues that made no sense on their own, then suddenly one scene comes along that makes everything clear at once? Did you get rush of insight and a slight buzz?

That's called an *epiphany*. Again, from the Greek word *"epiphaneia"*, epiphany means "appearance" or "manifestation. A moment of intense realization for the character and the Audience. If you manage your set ups properly, you can create them for the Audience in a way that makes them feel smart. The great director Ernst Lubitsch said: "Let the audience add up two plus two. They'll love you forever." You do this by layering set ups into the story and backstory. Set ups that, on their own don't seem to have a connection to anything in particular. They seem like trivia more than anything else.

Then, when the Audience is caught off guard, you hit them with a pay off that links all these set ups together in one simple fashion. The trick is to make it *simple*. Don't get too complex. Otherwise you'll create confusion instead of amazement.

The Audience can absorb a lot of information if it's given to them visually. This is why visual set ups and pay offs always work better than verbal ones. People have a tendency to rewrite conversations in their head. Words are also easily forgotten. But strong visuals stick.

So you hit them with images now and then that don't quite fit into the over all picture. Our attention is either drawn to these images for no apparent reason, or they stick out like a sore thumb in the midst of their scene. These cues are like road signs to the subconscious. They tell us "watch for falling rocks."

When I say images, this applies to prose as well. You describe what the character sees. You do it in such a way that it's memorable. Describing something boring won't do. If it's a banquet chair, for example, it has to have some unusual thing about it, like a ripped seat or a bent area. You have to use some special language to make it seem special in some way. So that it seems out of the ordinary. If you remember Chekov's shotgun over the fire place, a shotgun is ominous on its own. If it were a picture, you would need to describe it in such a way that people would remember it.

Then, in your key scene, you create the linkage. The Audience's mind will rush back through the story they have just experienced and all the pieces will fall together in a landslide. A rush of insight.

Pull off a trick like that and everyone will think you're a genius. But it's all the application of technique.

Setting up characters

This works in a similar way to the standard set up, but there are differences. Characters who play an important role later in the story need to be set up early on. But they also need to have a logical place in the relation of things.

In some stories a seemingly harmless character will turn out to be the true Villain, while earlier the Audience was tricked into thinking it was the guy with the hook. This is character set up through misdirection. The Audience doesn't mind that, and kind of expects it in some genres. The trick is never to make the true Villain too innocent and never make the false Villain too obvious. People will read a false Villain right away if he's too obvious. And a hidden Villain will stand out if he is too innocuous. It's better to give them faults, but a solid alibi so no one thinks it's them.

False Heroes are also useful set ups, as we saw in *South Pacific*. These characters are introduced in a way that makes them look like the strongest contender for the hero spot. They have a strong goal, they look and act right, everyone sees them as a leader in the story. But this is done to hide the real hero, who needs to emerge by the middle of the second act as a major player and a pivotal character. Usually false heroes are set up to be killed later so the real Hero is forced to make a crisis decision. In the GODFATHER, Michael Corleone had no intention of getting involved in the "family business." But when both his father and his brother are shot, no one else was qualified to take the reigns. He had to step in and become The Godfather.

Supporting characters need to be set up based on their eventual role in the story. An expert who helps the hero later in the story should be set up first. When heroes can pull experts out of the air it makes the story look bad.

It also looks bad when a character is set up that's an obvious device to help out the Hero. Like a explosive expert and lives and breathes his work and right away asks the hero when they can blow something up. You need to make sure these characters come across like real people and their talents are incidental. They can still be experts, though the term "the best in their field" is a cliché. So is saying someone belongs to "an elite team."

It's better to demonstrate how good someone is rather than tell it. If I told you I was the greatest writer who ever lived, you'd think I was a jerk or an ego maniac. It's highly unlikely you'd agree with me. People have to prove how good they. They can't just make boasts. And even their friend's boasting isn't enough on its own.

The same rule applies to characters. Saying someone is "the best" at what they do is not only an over used cliché, it's a put off. It's better to *show* how talented someone is, rather than tell.

Also, making someone "the best" at what they do weakens the conflict unless they're on the side of the

Villain. The hero shouldn't have the deck stacked in his favor. The Hero should have a hard time meeting his goals. Giving him too much ammunition is boring.

There is are exceptions to the set up principle, however. If something is set up or implied in the backstory or a character's backstory, it can be shown later, even if it's never been shown before. In *The Godfather II*, a character is introduced during the senate hearings against Michael Corleone. This character was never mentioned or shown before, but he gets Michael off the hook by just sitting in the background of the hearing and not saying a word. In fact, this character has no dialog in the film. But he works because he is implied in the backstory. The character is the brother of the man testifying against Michael Corleone. When the federal witness sees his brother in court, he recants his story against Corleone. Because one of the themes in the Godfather films is the importance of family, this character was set up by the theme. By implication rather than direct action.

This sort of pay off is acceptable and can lead to major surprises and plot twists. But it must be done carefully if you want it to work.

REMEMBER: Set up discreetly and pay off grandly.

INTRODUCTIONS

When your mother told you that first impressions go a long way, she was right. The first impression is what forms the Audience's opinion of a character. They will determine the character's alignment fairly quickly, based on their actions. You can use this to your advantage. But whatever you do, don't take first impressions for granted.

Characters need to be memorable. A story is always going to be about A>B<C. But the characters aren't always going to be the same. Characters are the most critical components of a story and they will make or break your work as surely as the structure will.

We discussed some of the things that make a character interesting. We discussed the different personality archetypes that people recognize. We discussed alignment. Now you have to put all of these things into practice.

When a character appears in the story, they have to do or say something that fixes our mind on who they are, what they're doing there, and what side of the conflict they fall on.

Their position in the story may change sides at any time. They can be protagonists who end up as antagonists. But we should have a good idea where they stand when they appear. Neutral characters are the story equivalent of fence sitters. The Audience isn't interested in them.

Characters need to be clear right away, because it tells us whether or not we should care about them when something happens. If you introduce a character, and they come off as neutral, or we're uncertain whether they are positive or negative in the story, and they get killed, we have no reason to care. And if we don't care, you've just set the mood for the story. Nothing matters.

The secret is finding the right balance of action and dialog that defines the character in a way that suits the scene and the plot at this point in the story. Characters change in a story, so it's okay to put across a different persona than what you intend later. All we need to know is should we like this character or not. And who are they and what are they doing here.

Character names should be given in a manner that is completely natural sounding. Fake sounding introductions are not the way to go, If a character has an odd name, having another character joke about it makes us not be so jarred when we hear it the first time. Such as, you have a character with a unusual ethnic name, and he corrects someone who gets it wrong.

People do use another's name in a conversation. But it never should sound forced.

It's also important to show the face of the person being introduced clearly. We need to put the face to the name. And the name and face should be reintroduced a couple more times in the story so we don't forget it. Therefore, you need to find fresh ways of getting their name to the Audience. Either by having them introduce themselves, or have them pointed out in some way, like in the news or by a person who recognizes them.

In prose, that means you describe a character and something unique about them so they are memorable. You only need to do this for important characters, not every character. You want to use imagery to describe them. This is a prose technique where you apply descriptive terms that evoke images in the reader's mind. Such as: "It was a dark night with no moon" evokes the feeling of gloom. "The aroma of fresh coffee filled the room." Evokes the smell of coffee. So it's making you imagine using your nose. You can play with all the senses using words to give us the imagined image that will be remembered later.

It's also helpful when a character is introduced in a memorable way. The master of this was the director Sergio Leone who opened *The Good, The Bad and the Ugly* with three sequences that gave us a very good sense of what the title characters were like. In the third sequence Clint Eastwood's character meets Tuco, Eli Wallach's character, and they begin an association that turns sour. The most powerful of these sequences is where Angel Eyes, Lee Van Cleef's character is introduced. He was the villain. The scene is so good that Quentin Tarantino made an homage to it in the opening of *Inglorious Basterds*.

A strong introduction makes a character seem important and memorable, which should be a goal.

CHARACTER ARC

This is a often misunderstood concept that's very important to the success of your story.

A character arc, also known as the character's journey, is about how a character changes in the course of a story. They should not be the same person they started out as at the end of it. Audiences expects a character to mature or change in some way. If that doesn't happen the story will feel empty to them. Pointless.

As I said before, people expect a story to have a point, to have meaning. The Hero of your story is their avatar. They need to identify or care about that Hero in some way and the arc is the way they care. We'll discuss how to make that arc work in the next chapter, but for now we should talk about the three types of arcs that a character will go on. Choose one to fit your story.

Change: This is the most classic arc. A normal guy, a everyman, is thrown into a whirlwind of adventures and he comes out the other side a hero. This is about a radical transformation of a character into a more confident or wise individual. The hero of this arc is mostly dealing with external conflicts and problems.

Growth: This is about a more reflective kind of personal growth. A character has to overcome their own inner demons (fear, insecurity, etc) in order to master external problems and in the process becomes a better, stronger person.

Fall: This is the opposite of the other two arcs. This is about how a character fails. The mistakes they make that ends up being their undoing. These kinds of stories are tragedies and their endings are not happy in any way.

Character Arc refers to the Hero's learning curve in a

story. A Hero starts off with certain attitudes and beliefs and by the end of the story they come away with new insights and direction in life. The Hero may also grow and mature through the course of their adventure, becoming a better or worse person than when they started. They can become more wise, more knowledgeable.

Some people have theorized that the secret to characterization is to first figure out what you want your character to learn, then start them off at the exact opposite of that conclusion. This isn't a bad theory since it also plays hand in hand with the premise concept. But we all know there is more to characterization than that.

It's far too simple to have a character go from bad to good in a story. We all know that people fall back on old habits easily. Someone may clean up their act today, but come Sunday they're back to drinking sterno. Your story has to convince us that the character has truly seen the light, if that's what your goal is.

Unfortunately, it's extremely trite to take a character who has views in direct opposition to your own and make them take your side by the end. People don't like having morality or political opinions shoved down their throats. Especially if they disagree with them. And Audience's can tell when the writer is setting up a character to make some moral point that match's the writer's views.

You can pull this off if you make the counter premise extremely compelling. To do this you need to understand the other side of the argument well and realize all the good points the other side makes. By working through all the arguments of the counter premise in your story, you can then establish in a sound, reasonable way, the foundation for your version of the truth.

But character arc isn't limited to political or social issues. A character can learn to be sober. They can learn to be better fishermen. Better mathematicians. In the classic Japanese film *Tampopo*, it was about a young woman becoming a better noodle chef. You can make the goal of the character arc anything you want. In the film *Rocky*, the character had to go from insecure and unfocused to determined and confident. That was his arc. The arc relates to the various levels of conflict you're dealing with. You take the character from one value to another.

One of the worse mistakes writers make when dealing with character arc is having the character explain at the end what they've learned. This should be self evident. It should be demonstrated. Having a character mouth platitudes is not only preachy, it's insincere. We see this in a lot of older TV shows. *South Park* even works with that convention but they usually do it in a way that's farcical.

As we discussed earlier, anyone can say they've learned something. It's like saying "I'm sorry". It's just words. It doesn't mean there is any truth in it. We need to see the arc demonstrated clearly and the Audience should know, for certain, that this character has learned what they had to learn, without being told.

Truth is something we need to see in practice. It's the old Missouri principle. Seeing is believing. Demonstrate in a clear and powerful way that your character is seeing and acting differently, and that they are doing so because they learned to do so.

Whatever you do, don't just have them say it. No one will believe them. Too many of us know the meaning of codependent from experience. We know how hard it is for people to change.

Villains can arc, but don't always need to. If you do a story where the Villain starts off good, but becomes evil by the end of the story, that's his arc. But you need to establish strong reasons for this arc to make his journey believable. This can be done using story values, which is a subject we'll discuss next.

The TV series *Breaking Bad* is famous for its character arc of turning a good man into a despised villain. It's a great example of fall arc done over six seasons.

Major supporting characters should arc in relation to the hero. This gives the story dimension. But the supporting characters arcs don't need to be as grand as the heroes. And their arcs should have something to do with the events in the story.

The focus of the character arc is always going to be the Hero. His arc is the main point of the story, in most cases. Stories are about change. The hero needs to change in some way. Obviously, in a monthly comic book, you can't affect an arc every storyline. So you should consider making the main character secondary and arcing someone else. Or you should create stakes that imply a change for the Hero's life that implies an arc of some kind, even if he doesn't change.

Whatever you do, don't arc a Hero away from the things that make him work as a hero. You don't want Batman to become a happy, well adjusted person. You don't want Superman to become a vengeful maniac. Character's should remain true to themselves. You just want to arc them in a way that validates the premise, but doesn't invalidate them as a workable hero.

REMEMBER: Show, don't Tell. The character arc must be demonstrated clearly.

STORY VALUES

If there is anything in this book stands out as the most useful bit of technique you can learn, this is it. Story Values.

Everything else in this book is important or useful. But this is a concept that truly revolutionizes your work and sets it above the pack. Story values are how you demonstrate character arcs. It's how you demonstrate change. It's how you make a story seem like it squeezed the last drop of passion out of the conflict.

Story values are the levels a conflict can pass through. They are the limits of human experience. You need to take the Hero through all the levels of human experience to craft a completely satisfying tale. Once you understand these levels, you can then set the goals you need to meet by the story's end.

Values are the points on a curve any given status or emotional state of being can take. There are four levels of story values: Positive, Compromised, Negative, Detrimental. Let's examine what these are. When I list the examples below, they will be in six categories. The next set of examples show you their alternates on the curve.

Positive: This is the value we all want our life to be experiencing. It's when things are great. Everything is coming up roses. You're at the top of the heap. Examples of positive values are: Love, Wealthy, Justice, Truth, Healthy, Free.

Compromised: When you enter this plane of values, things are on the skids. You're on a downward spiral but haven't hit bottom yet. Things could also get better. Examples: Indifference, Broke, Unfairness, White Lies, Sick, Constrained.

Negative: When you hit bottom, this is where you enter the territory of the Negative values. It's the skids, the pits, etc. This is a destructive value, but not the most destructive. Things could still get worse. But worse is something you don't even want to think about. Examples: Hate, Bankrupt, Injustice, Lies, Dead, Imprisoned.

Detrimental: If Negative is when you hit bottom, Detrimental is when the bottom falls out from under you. Once you've hit the realm of detrimental, you can only lose or win. There's no other way to go. You've reached the end of the line. Examples: Hate masquerading as love, In debt to a murderous loanshark, Tyranny, Self Deception, Undead, In a Concentration camp.

Exploring the Values

Let's see how they work in terms of a story. The hero is our milk loving friend Kyle. The villain is a loan shark named Rafe.

WEALTHY: Our hero Kyle starts off a wealthy man. But due to something that happens during the Trigger Event he becomes flat broke during the first Turning point. He spends the second act trying to get himself back on top, so he takes out loans to gamble in Vegas, hoping to win the money he needs to end up where he was before. That's his goal in the story. But Kyle keeps losing during the progressive complication stage and his credit is cut off. He's run out of money. He's bankrupt. No one will lend to him. No one but Rafe, a loan shark. Kyle takes the loan from Rafe. But he loses the money and can't pay Rafe back. Now Rafe is actively looking for Kyle. He plans to either break his legs or kill him as an example. Kyle only has one quarter left to his name. He gambled his last few bucks on the slots. As he turns to leave the Casino Kyle sees Rafe across the room, looking at him. Rafe's men are with him and they move to block all the exits. Rafe approaches Kyle with deadly intent. Kyle has nowhere to run. We've now reached the climax.

The story began with Kyle being wealthy, the positive extreme. We took the values down to an extreme low of being in debt to a psycho. Imagine how effective this would play, fleshed out with characterization and plot twists.

Now we can choose between three possible endings. Up, Down, or Ironic. These will determine which path Kyle's life will end up on.

UP: Kyle puts his last quarter in a slot machine as Rafe and his men walk toward him. Desperate, Kyle pulls the lever. He sees Rafe draw his gun. Suddenly, lights and alarms go off. Rafe stops in his tracks, surprised. Kyle turns to look at the slot machine. He's just won the big pay off! Two million dollars! Kyle is rich again! Rafe puts away his gun and says: "Congratulations."

DOWN: Kyle puts his last quarter in a slot machine as Rafe and his men walk toward him. Desperate, Kyle pulls the lever. He sees Rafe draw his gun. Rafe's expression turns from bad to worse as he draws close and jabs the gun against Kyle's back. Kyle turns to look at the slot. He lost. RAFE: "You had your chance, Kyle. Now you're going for a ride!" Rafe's men grab Kyle's arms and he's dragged off into the night.

IRONIC: Kyle puts his last quarter in a slot machine as Rafe and his men walk toward him. Desperate, Kyle pulls the lever. He sees Rafe draw his gun. Suddenly, lights and alarms go off. Rafe stops in his tracks, surprised. Kyle turns to look at the slot. He's just won the big pay off. $100,000. Exactly the amount of money he owes Rafe. Rafe puts his gun away and almost smiles. Kyle wipes the sweat from his brow. He's still broke, and in debt to other people, but at least he doesn't owe Rafe anymore. Just then, three security guards show up with a man in a cheap suit. The man says: "I'm Mr. Finster from the I.R.S. You'll have to pay the income tax on that money." Rafe can't make a move with the guards there, so he leaves. Kyle knows he's been given some extra time. Will it be enough?

TRUTH: We can add on more values to the same story by choosing those which are complimentary to the plot. Same exact story, but here's how more values adds to the plot. Kyle's a successful man with his own business. He's level headed. He's honest and fair. But he needs a big deal to make his business more successful and he tells a white lie to a potential client. This is the Trigger event. The white lie not only costs Kyle the deal, but he's also sued by the client. He loses the law suit during the Turning Point of act one and becomes broke. During the second act he borrows money, using false information (lies) to get the loans. When this is discovered his credit is cut off, so he starts gambling. As he loses, he goes into denial, telling himself he is going to win it all back. And he lies to himself right up until the end, wanting to believe that success is just around the corner. This is a classic Fall arc.

As you see, the values serve several roles. They establish the levels of conflict. They are the basis of motivation and causation. They raise the stakes in the story.

When you use values to go from one extreme to the other, you build a powerful charge. And when the climax occurs you have things at such an extreme point, that reversing everything in one final act, righting all the wrongs, setting things back to where the hero wants them to be, creates a feeling of great exhilaration for the Audience. Or it makes the Ironic ending funny. Or it makes the negative ending devastating.

Notice how the values are married to the causal effect. The Audience needs to see that actions have consequences. They expect the Newtonian rules of physics to apply to a story. When you do one thing, it causes another thing to occur. This principle creates a feeling of realism.

So we use values to add more and more power to the conflict(s) of the story. We can tie together three or four sets of values easily. Even more if we have to. And by doing so we create a feeling of believability and complexity in the work. We also make the story meaningful.

When a character goes through the limits of human experience, they *really* discover the meaning of the word "adventure."

REMEMBER: Take us through the values and we'll feel the full range of human experience.

DEFINING MOMENTS

These are scenes that tell us in a demonstrative way what kind of person a character is. This goes back to what I was saying about Introductions, but sometimes you might want to save the defining moment for a key scene.

The defining moment is critical to establishing the character firmly in our minds. They need to happen at least twice for the Hero and once for every major character. The purpose of these scenes is to let us know where our hero stands. You do not want an evasive, wishy-washy hero. You need to demonstrate how strongly they stand by their principals. If they don't, you risk making them look weak.

Early in the story we need a scene to tell us where the hero is at the beginning of his arc. By the end of the story we need another to show where he is at the end of the arc. For the hero, that final defining moment should be during the climax.

For Villains, the defining moment is based on what the Audience perception of the Villain is supposed to be in the story. If the Villain is a false protagonist throughout most of the story, you need to define him as such until you reach the point where you are going to pull off their mask. Then, you hit the audience with a defining moment that shows us what the Villain's true feelings are. An excellent example of this can be seen in the Alfred Hitchcock film Shadow of a Doubt. In this film Joseph Cotten plays a character named "Uncle Charley" who everyone loves, including the heroine of the story, his niece. But throughout the course of the story, the niece begins to realize something isn't right with her uncle. She begins to suspect him of being a serial killer. There's a dinner scene where Uncle Charley starts talking about widows and what he thinks of them. This scene is a perfect example of a defining moment.

Another excellent example can be found in the graphic novel *Watchmen* by Alan Moore and Dave Gibbons. In the first issue, Rorschach, the false hero of the story, enters a seedy bar to get information. When he enters the bar the bartender first nervously welcomes Rorschach and then...almost in the same breath, says: "Please don't hurt anyone!"

This scene shows us how Rorschach is perceived by the public at large. It's a defining moment using other characters to define the central character. This is an alternate technique to reach the same goal.

Defining moments make the story more exciting. They add to the power of a story by delivering a gut punch at just the right time. These are the moments you really want to learn how to pull off well. They will help make your story all the more enjoyable.

REMEMBER: Defining moments help make your characters come alive.

POINT OF VIEW (P.O.V.)

There are times in a story you may want to show what the character sees through their own eyes. this is known as a POV or Point of View. This technique serves two purposes. It puts us in the head of the character so we can experience life the way they are at that given moment in time. It also shows us a different perspective on the story than we may have been experiencing.

In prose, George RR Martin used the POV technique for multiple characters in his *Song of Ice and Fire* books (aka *Game of Thrones*). Each chapter would provide the POV of one character and would show the world of the story as they see it. This let you get into the head of that character and experience things from their perspective.

In film we've seen the Cam shot where a camera is pot on something and everything is shown from that perspective. Often it is used to show a distressed version of the character's POV as they are having some kind of emotional crisis.

In comics, it's not unusual to have the art in the panels reflect what a character sees with the character's running commentary about it all. Daniel Clowes' comic *Eightball* had a short story called *The Walk* where everything that was shown was from the perspective of a character we don't see. And the narration was the angry commentary running through that characters head. His commentary was judgmental or frustrated by whatever he saw. It was a very effective and funny approach to a classic technique.

POVs are not limited to visual points of reference. We can do an external POV. This is done by having the character narrate the story and what we are shown is how the character interprets the action. The character also narrates the story from their personal perspective and world view.

Neil Gaiman used this approach effectively in his *Miracleman* "The Golden Age" stories. Non superhuman people were observing the affects superhumans had on their lives. This technique was later used in *Marvels*, by Kurt Busiek and Alex Ross to much acclaim.

The secret of POVs is remembering that it's not your view as the writer, but the *character's* personal view based on their limitations, opinions, attitudes, and perspective. It can be used as a characterization device, or it can be used as a means to show the horrible situation a character is in. It can be used to show how appalling the character's mind set is. Or how good it is.

When you write from a character's POV, you must understand the character as if they were you. You must believe what they believe as you write them. You must become that character for a time, even if that character is a complete anathema to you. If you're a black writer doing a story from the POV of a Klansman, you need to understand the Klansman's views as if they were your own. You actually have to allow yourself to believe it as you write so that the character comes across as real. If you're a white writer doing a story from the POV of a Native American during the Indian Wars, you need to understand the perspective of the red man and their culture and why they feel that way. You have to avoid all the stereotypes you've seen in movies and go for the truth.

As we discussed in the chapter on Villains, everyone sees themselves as the hero of their own story. But as a writer, you have the opportunity to show the errors in their thinking through their POV. You are allowing the Audience to get in their head through your words.

Even if you agree with the character you are writing from POV, you need to make sure they come off as human with flaws. Otherwise, you're being nothing more than a tour guide pointing out sights along the way. We need insight during a POV. We need to understand what makes the character tick. We don't need the same old same old.

POV should never be wasted on generic views or scenes, because it's a very personal technique. It puts the Audience into the mind of the character. If you establish the experience as straightforward and uneventful, the audience will quickly become bored because they are seeing nothing to make the experience worthwhile.

REMEMBER: POV is not your view, it's the character's.

SUB-PLOTS

Sub-plots are miniature stories within the main body of your story. They exist to develop events and characters that are taking place outside the experience of the Hero. Sub plots are especially helpful in keeping the middle part of the story interesting.

Aristotle said that plots must have a beginning, middle, and end, and that each event in the plot causes the next event to happen. A sub-plot is just a plot within a plot. A story within a story. But it exists to expand on and enrich your overall story by telling something that happens concurrently with it.

It's wise to treat sub-plots like one or two act stories. But we usually don't get to see the whole act at once. Often a sub-plot begins with a trigger event and develops to a crisis, but we don't see the climax until later in the story where it affects the main plot.

Sub-plots can be broken up in three or four places. We can cut back to them where they left off as needed. But each scene or sequence involving a sub plot should work smoothly with the main body of the story.

There are two kinds of sub-plots. The set up sub-plot serves to set up the Trigger Event for the main story. The complication sub-plot exists to develop the story in the second act by throwing on another progressive complication.

Complication sub-plots are extremely important. They can not only add dimension to your story, they can also be used to contradict the premise and create irony. They can be used to develop supporting characters. They show us events going on outside the main body of the story which are related.

They allow you to play variations on a theme. You can use them to make your story resonate. Even though they are part of your main story, you can use them as counter stories, telling variations of the main tale in order to show the diversity of life.

Sub-plots can give you a lot of possibilities, but you need to make sure they flow seamlessly within the main work. You don't want discordant melodies running amok.

The beauty of the sub plot is that you can tell a story with a different theme to fill in some event or backstory inside your over all tale. If you remember the chapter on story shapes, you can imagine how the beginning, middle and end play out You an tell multiple stories in one master work using the sub-plot.

REMEMBER: Sub-plots help add dimension and resonance.

REVERSALS

When we try to perform a task, things don't always happen the way we expect them to. In many cases, the opposite result occurs. It's called a reversal. You go to do something important and you're prevented from doing it because of something else that prevents you. In many ways, its like the protagonist vs the antagonist. But in a story it can be many things and it's best if it surprises the audience.

A classic example, which is admittedly over used, is where the hero has to escape some monster or killers, so they get in their car to drive away and it won't start. Such a scene works because most people have encountered this problem in real life, sans the monsters and killers. A car not starting when you want it to is a annoying problem. Made even worse by the treat to your life, in the case of a story. It ramps up the tension which is why this trope has been used in a lot of movies and TV show (not to mention books).

In your story, the hero will try to take the path of least resistance. You can't allow him to get away with that. If everything he tries works the way he wants it to, the story will be uneventful and dull. On the other hand, you need to make the reversals believable. If you have a hero jump in his car to chase the Villain and it doesn't start, you need to set up car problems first. If the car looks like a junker, that's all the set up you need. But a new car should start. People expect a certain amount of realism.

Reversals work best when they are part of an elaborate set up. You build immense anticipation in the audience as the hero goes to perform a task. And when he tries it seems to work for a second, but then--POW! Major complications result.

The opening sequence of *Raiders of the Lost Ark* is a good example of this. Indiana Jones has to deal with all sorts of problems and death traps to get into an ancient temple so he can take a golden idol that's hidden deep within. He fills a bag with sand to try to approximate the weight of the idol. He switches the bag with the idol and everything seems to be cool. No problems. He turns to leave and that's when it becomes apparent he screwed up. Now he's under real pressure to save himself. Before he could take his time evading the death traps. Now he has to run for it and hope he doesn't get killed.

Reversals should only be the beginning of a set of repercussions and further reversals. You're trying to apply Murphy's Law ("Anything that can go wrong, will go wrong.") to your story, but you need to do it in a way the audience can believe.

In bad fiction we've seen reversals that seem to be arbitrary plot devices. They aren't Murphy's Law in action. They feel more like Sturgeon's Law ("95% of everything is crap!"). If a complicated reversal occurs, we need the set up. It can be subtle, but we must be clued in as to why the reversal may have happened.

Another form of reversal is the telegraphed reversal. In this one, the audience knows the hero is going to fail when he throws that switch or opens that door because the Audience was cued that it wouldn't work earlier. But the hero doesn't know that. The story first sets up the hero's plans, then shows in a sub-plot that the villain or an antagonist already anticipated this move and has countered it. So when the hero tries to do something he thinks will work, it blows up in his face. Because the audience was told to expect this, they are filled with dread before the hero makes his move. They might even scream at the page "Don't do it!" This technique is very useful in

191

suspense stories.

Reversals also have another advantage. They can be used as a tool to show character growth as part of the character's journey. When your character finds that something doesn't work, they can show how smart they are by creatively thinking a way out of their predicament. And you can use this as an opportunity to show them learning something new. Something that helps them develop so they gain wisdom or strength. Reversals aren't just annoying things that happen to a character, they can be life lessons that help them advance. And for the reader, that can be meaningful.

REMEMBER: Reversals create a feeling of realism, but only if they're believable.

CONTRAST

This technique is used to highlight the differences between characters, thus defining them in sharp, easy to understand ways. It can also be used to highlight your main character so he stands out from the pack.

In film, the use of color is often used for contrast. The background and costume colors are chosen very carefully. Study films and you'll see one color scheme used in the entire film. In comics, you may have no control over the coloring, so it's best to deal with contrast through writing. In prose, contrast is done through characterization.

As we discussed before there are recognizable personality archetypes. And in addition to that certain people bring out certain qualities in our personalities. When you create a scene, it's a good idea to use characters that do not blend with each other. You want the characters to seem different. Visuals aren't enough.

In life, we're pressured by society and others to conform. Many of us resist it, but we still try to conform in some ways. It's human nature to try to be part of the herd. If you don't conform to some model of normalcy, you won't get laid. And that's a major motivation right there. But conformity is unacceptable in fiction. Characters need to contrast with one another so we can see why they're so different and unique from each other. If you don't do that you create what people call "cookie cutter characters." Characters that seem to all be from the same mold and that is *really* boring.

Some writers, when given a job they aren't enthused about, or if they're in a hurry to meet a deadline, often write characters with the same voice, have them act in a predictable fashion, and even though these characters are normally unique, they become generic as if they were cookie cutter characters. You have to avoid that impulse.

This is something to be extremely aware of and to avoid at all costs. You want characters to bounce off each other. You want them to annoy and be amused and cajole and connive each other. You need to get into the heads of each character and see through their eyes. The last thing you want is for everyone to get along too well. People can be the best of friends, but they will disagree on some things. And as a writer you have the power to decide to make that part of the conversation to highlight their differences.

In some old TV sit-coms like Leave it to Beaver, everyone got along more or less in the family. But each character was distinct and different from each other. They had attributes that made them special. Even in the Brady Bunch.

So discover what it is that makes a character special and play it off the other characters. It's its liable to rub one character the wrong way, all the better. In *Star Trek,* Spock always upset McCoy because McCoy was a man of feeling and Spock was a man of intellect. Their archetypes were the Sage and Mr. Sensitive. Spock was a scientist, so he was mainly an intellectual person. McCoy was a doctor, so he was a man with empathy for others. He hated to see someone look at everything from an aloof perspective (Spock also had a bit of the Lord archetype in him). If you threw in Kirk who was a cross between the Hero and the Harlot, you had a potent mix.

Character dynamics are really important to understand because they can inspire you to create great conversations. When you're writing a scene between two characters with completely different world views, they almost write themselves. Those traits within yourself start to speak you start writing like a demon. It's a very satisfying feeling when this happens because you know you're on to something. You're writing from the heart.

There are three types of contrast characters worth knowing. These three characters are often used in fiction to great effect.

The Straight Man

If you're familiar with comedy teams, you're familiar with the straight man. The straight man is the "normal one" who ends up taking the brunt of the humor from the comical character he's paired with. Abbott and Costello, Lewis and Martin, Laurel and Hardy, even the comedy teams like the Three Stooges and the Marx Brothers used straight men. They would either find an external straight man or one of the team members would play the role.

If you've seen *Warner Brothers* cartoons, you know that Elmer Fudd is the straight man. Sometimes Daffy Duck, who in solo stories plays the Comic, ends up the straight man when paired in stories with Bugs. For comedy to work you need someone who gets mad, who's straight, to play the comedy off of.

But you don't need to do comedy to use a straight man. Straight men are symbols of normalcy, some element of society or the status quo. We all get mad at the system. We all get sick of normalcy. Straight men are the punching bags for writers to work their angst on. But they need to be characters we can relate to on some level. They have to be recognizable types of people.

The Gadfly

This character serves as the thorn in the side. The itch you can't scratch. The trouble-maker you'd like to see go away, but who won't. This are great characters to have in stories because they are the source of conflict. They keep things going. You just have to make sure you don't over do it with these guys.

Gadflies can be likable characters, but they rub certain

195

people the wrong way and they cause problems for others either by being irresponsible, clumsy, impulsive, anything that can lead to trouble.

Dr. Smith in *Lost in Space* was a gadfly character. The only problem was, they ended up making him a straight man after awhile because they over used him. Gadflies need to be used in the right circumstances and never over exposed. You can dilute their effectiveness that way.

There's also this annoying tendency writers have lately, of trying to "improve" gadflies. They try to take away all the qualities that make them what they are. This robs them of their usefulness in a story. The idea is to make them a better person.

Newsflash: We don't want to read about better people. We want to read about jerks.

Wolverine was a gadfly in the *X-Men*. He didn't fit in. He was a loner. He was a trouble-maker. He would fight with the other members all the time. And then the writers decided, hey...let's make him more lovable. He shouldn't be so angry and violent.

Marvel ended up killing him off.

The world isn't composed of entirely of nice, well adjusted people. The world is composed of all kinds of people, many of whom are a serious pain in the ass. Even the nice people you want to strangle sometimes.

And in fiction, the point is to create conflict. One way you do that is to throw in characters that stir things up. That make people angry. That people get upset with. Those characters may be hated by the audience, but they will do wonders for your story. Because if the audience ends up hating people they're supposed to dislike, you're half way home.

The Mentor

When you have a hero who is basically an uneducated

fool, or who is young and reckless, the mentor is a good way to educate him. The mentor is the teacher, the role model, the parent figure who helps your character through his arc. The mentor doesn't always have to be obviously a mentor. They can play the role subtlety. And they don't have to be likable or smooth even. Stick, *Daredevil's* mentor in the Frank Miller stories was a grouchy old man who used to hit Matt Murdock on the head. Mister Miyage in the *Karate Kid* seemed like an abusive conman until we got to see what he was doing. In *Kill Bill,* Pai Mei, Gordon Lui's character is the cruel racist teacher of The Bride (Uma Thurman's character). He is unlikeable but he helps her become a stronger person. We only find out later he teaches her a secret he has taught no one else. Those are all martial arts characters but you could see similar versions in movies about dancing or sports. In an *Officer and a Gentleman,* Lou Gossett Jr. Is the mentor to Richard Gere's military character. In *Batman Begins* it's Ducard (Liam Neeson's character) who trains Batman and is later revealed to be the villain.

Just make sure the mentor is believable and has something worthwhile to say. But they should never be perfect. People don't buy that. And they are generally wary of parent figures in stories.

REMEMBER: Contrast highlights character differences and makes for sharper writing.

ACTION

Action and conflict are two separate things. Action is the result of conflict. Conflict is the reason for most action.

Many writers think they are the same thing. So they put fights and explosions in their stories as a substitute for meaningful conflict. Audiences walk away from these stories feeling empty. In their heart of hearts they know what they just saw was fireworks, nothing more. There was nothing to remember or care about except for some flashing lights.

When action is used as a substitute for conflict, you have a meaningless story Oscar Wilde said it best: "The basis of action is lack of imagination. It is the last resource of those who know not how to dream." Action does serve a purpose, but it should never be used as a device just to keep the story moving along. The true source of momentum isn't action scenes. Don't forget that.

When you set out to write action scenes, you need to create a sense of causality. We either need to see what lead up to this action, or we need to understand why it's happening if we're thrown in the middle of it. As we discussed before, we need to know who to root for. We need to have a sense of why we should care about any of this. It can't be just a bunch of flying bullets and crashing cars. Everyone has seen that a million times. What they really want are good reasons for it all.

Action scenes also need to flow in a realistic manner. Too often we get action scenes that have poor motivation and don't make any sense when you follow them.Physics is a real life rule of nature that often gets ignored in movies and comic books. But unrealistic action can throw off the Audience and make them lose their bond.

Action scenes, in order to be effective, need to have an

emotional impact as well as a physical one. There must be some kind of repercussions. There must be stakes for the hero and the villain. When you create an action scene, think through all the possible combinations of outcomes. Write them down. Then pick the ideas that are the most original and surprising.

Also remember that action needs to define the characters, because the choices they make in these actions scenes illustrate the way their mind works under pressure.

Medias Res

This means "In the Middle of things". It's a term used mainly for a technique of starting a story in the middle the action. A lot of films and books like to begin media res. It allows the creators to show the different characters in action, so we can see what their powers and abilities are. The secret to making such scenes work is to define who the protagonists are right away. You need to establish this by having them demonstrate their alignment.

It's far too common these days to read stories where 50 characters are all in a big battle, shouting each others names out loud so we know who is who. But never are we given any insight into the characters themselves. The most we get to know is what side they're on. Even little kids want more than that. Audiences need characters they can root for.

Since action in comics is basically a series of still shots of things happening, you need to make it really clear what is happening in each panel and you have to keep it simple. The more detail, the more the reader will be distracted. The more distracted, the longer it takes for them to read the panel. The more time it takes, the slower the scene feels.

In film, there has to be a clarity to the storytelling or people will get bored by the sensory overload. Too many

CGI epics have this problem where the director made the mistake of thinking special effects will automatically make it cool. No, it doesn't. What makes a scene cool is when its well crafted and coherent.

In prose everything needs to flow in a matter that makes sense. If you want to produce a "fog of war" effect where it's all confusing, you will have to make scenes that follow break down what happened.

Action scenes need to be exciting. So they must have a high emotional charge and they must play fast and loose. Too much dialog and we start to lose steam. The goal should be to build steam. Because the action scene should work toward it's own climax.

So, when jumping into a scene, Medias Res, remember that you start with momentum, and you need to build toward a pay off. That pay off is the climax of the scene. And the pay off will work a lot better if we get some set up first. We need to know who is who, what is what and why the hell is all this going on.

There will be some instances where you want mystery in the scene, but we still need to know who to root for, even if it turns out to be the wrong person later. If we're given no reasons to care, we won't. And you don't want the Audience to start off the story feeling indifferent.

REMEMBER: Action needs meaning. Conflict is the meaning behind all action.

TEXT AND SUBTEXT

In a nutshell, Text is what you see, Subtext is the hidden meaning behind it. Or, if you prefer a more intellectual explanation, text is the tactile, surface experience of the story. Subtext is the inner life of the story. The subconscious.

If you want to be a good writer, you need to get a handle on subtext. Because no good writer writes "on the nose." Writing on the nose means what the character says is exactly what the character means. Everything is textual.

In real life, people do not say exactly what they mean most of the time. In fact, some people are incapable of it. Bad fiction is full of dialog where the characters say precisely what's on their mind and precisely what they really think. It doesn't work like that in most cases. Most people have learned to hide their true thoughts and you have to read between the lines to get what they're really saying.

But subtext isn't limited to dialog. It can be part of a situation. Situations can have hidden meaning. So can objects in a room. So can the choice of clothes someone wears. If a woman dresses sexy the subtext could be she's looking to get attention, and/or laid. If a man dresses in a suit, it means he's about business of some kind.

An example of situational subtext can be found in the movie *Disclosure,* when Demi Moore's character invites Michael Douglas up to her office after hours. It's a business meeting where she tries to seduce him. But even more is going on there than meets the eye. She's also trying to set him up.

In *Batman Returns*, Bruce Wayne shows Dick Grayson his motorcycle collection. The subtext of this scene is he's trying to seduce Grayson into staying at the mansion. The dialog in this scene is full of subtext.

A truly great film to study for sub-text is *There Will Be Blood*. Daniel Plainview (Daniel Day Lewis) is a oil speculator who buys up land cheaply by making all sorts of promises to the people who own the land. He pretends to be this moral character and family man. But when you watch those scenes he is basically letting the people he is conning talk and then he only says what he has to to get them to agree with his deal. At first you might buy is act, but later you find out what a psycho he really is. He has complete contempt for other people and seems to enjoy buying their oil on the cheap. This is helped a lot by the great acting but the writing is where it all comes from.

We'll deal with sub-textual dialog in depth later, but just remember for now that you can create more meaning in a story by using subtext. And with dialog, it makes it more realistic if you dance around the direct meaning of the words.

Audiences need to be drawn in to a story on a participation level. Subtext gives them the means to do that. They start to fill in the blanks with their mind and this makes them more engaged. You need the means to do this because comics limits you with its visuals. In prose, the reader's mind creates images based on the words of the writer. It's a very personal thing for each reader. In comics, they see what the artist has represented as the actual appearance of things. This limits their imagination. They don't have to become too engaged in the work. So in order to make them more engaged, we need psychological tricks to draw them in more. Subtext is one of those methods.

Text, that which is obvious, serves as the surface reality beyond which our minds need to penetrate. Subtext is the prize we get for making the effort.

REMEMBER: Subtext creates meaning for the Audience.

CHANCE AND COINCIDENCE

This is very dangerous territory, however it can be useful. Things that happen by chance or coincidence can be used to provide meaning to a story. But they can also make your story look ridiculous if used improperly.

Coincidence is a popular device in comedy, because it's somewhat preposterous. It happens in real life, but rarely. So if it happens a lot in a story, it's absurd, and thus can be used for comic effect.

It's perfectly acceptable to begin a story with a coincidence. People believe they can happen. And coincidence brings across the feeling that fate is involved. So using coincidence to start a story can add a certain symbolic charge. But in serious fiction, it should *never* be used to end a story. Coincidence not only robs the hero of his shining moment, it never happens when you need it to happen. The audience won't buy a coincidental ending.

It generally should never be used throughout a story. Unless you want to establish the premise that life is absurd. By using chance or coincidence as a causality for major events, you pain the picture that life is nuts. But this should be done carefully and it's better handled in comedic stories.

In most cases chance and coincidence are used as cheap plot devices by writers who are stuck with what to do next. I'll do a mea culpa here and admit to having committed this sin myself. But it's something to be avoided. Audiences have become very sophisticated over the years having been exposed to so many books, comics, TV shows and films. They are very familiar with good and bad writing. They can spot a weak plot a mile away.

Chance and coincidence may happen in real life, but in fiction, people find it hard to swallow unless you use it in

204

certain ways. The Greek philosopher Heraclitus stated that "Character is Destiny". We all have a feeling in our lives, especially in our youth, that we have some sort of destiny before us, good or bad. Chance represents the hand of fate to many people. This is why Shakespeare was able to get away with using it so much in his play *Othello*. The play makes us feel Othello had a destiny to fulfill and fate was going to make sure it happened.

When chance and coincidence is used in favor of the hero, the audience doesn't usually believe it. But when it's used against the hero, it seems more realistic. In our gambling story, for example, if Kyle won the money in the story the way we supposed in the up ending, it would be unacceptable to a lot of people, because that's just too unbelievable. But the ending where he loses, or the ironic ending where he loses his gains is far more "realistic". This is because the odds are usually against us.

REMEMBER: Never end a story with a coincidence and keep chance to a minimum.

MISDIRECTION

The Audience resents cheap surprises. They don't like it when you throw arbitrary things at them. But they do like it when you surprise them with in an intelligent way. One technique for doing this is called Misdirection. You make them think one thing is going to happen, then you surprise them with something else instead.

This has to be done correctly, though. Too many bad movies have used this technique in a shoddy way. Everyone has seen the frightened woman who feels she's being stalked by a murderer. She stupidly walks into a dark room and doesn't see the shadowy figure hiding in plain sight, which springs out at her....and turns out to be her goofy boyfriend. The audience relaxes their guard for a second and then the real murderer leaps at them from another dark part of the room and kills them both!

Misdirection doesn't need to involve psycho killers. It can be used for everything. It's a form of a reversal, but it's a double whammy because it's not just a reversal for a character in the story, it's a reversal of the Audience's expectations.

You set something up so the Audience expects "A" to happen. But then, when "A" is supposed to happen you hit them with "B" instead. But "B" has to be set up first. It can't just come out of nowhere. I has to be a believable event.

Therefore, you set up "A" so it looks like "A" is inevitable. Like it's a sure thing. And subtly, you set up "B" in a completely innocuous way. Sometimes setting up "B" can be avoided if it's something that's inherently natural to the situation. To use the bad example set above. If the Audience is expecting the psycho killer to be lurking behind the door and it's just the goofy boyfriend, that's a natural (though annoying) event. The goofy boyfriend has to be introduced to the story first, of course.

Let's say the story involves a car race across country and the villain has sprayed an oil slick ahead of the hero that he's unaware of. It's around a corner, so by the time you see it, its too late to stop. Earlier, another car hit the slick and crashed. It exploded and sent metal shards all over the road. The audience will expect something similar to happen to the hero's car. But instead, the hero's car runs over the metal shards and gets two flats. Because the tires are flat, the car is able to keep some sort of traction and is able to pass the slick safely.

The key is to bury the set up for action "B" in a way that doesn't seem obvious. When the car explodes, the audience should think it's just part of the action of the story, but as we discussed, there should be repercussions for each action.

REMEMBER: Misdirection must be set up as a double whammy, not as a cheap surprise.

SCENE TRANSITIONS

This chapter mainly deals with visual medium like comics or film. In prose you can do this with words if it strikes your fancy.

When a scene ends, you need to move on to the next one in a smooth fashion so the Audience isn't jarred out of the spell you've hopefully laid on them. Scene Transitions are the technique for doing this.

There are three basic ways to make a scene transition. One is visual, one is textual, the other is random (also known as the "Jump cut"). Visual transitions involve linking images through thematic or symbolic parallels. Textual transitions bridge the two scenes with copy. Random transitions just throw you into another situation with no apparent linkage.

Let's look at some examples:

Visual

Here's a scene from an imaginary film or comic. A man drinking tea outside is shot, His tea cup shatters on the ground, the tea splattering. The next shot is later, the man's blood pools under his dead body as the camera pulls back to show a forensics technician drawing a chalk outline while another is dusting for prints in the background. Dialog: "Looks like he was killed about three hours ago."

In the above sequence we've witnessed a man get murdered. This is followed by a new scene sometime later when the body is found. The forensics man's dialog tells us the estimated time jump. The thematic linking device is spilled fluid. We see the shattered cup symbolizing destruction, the spilled tea symbolizing blood. We cut to a shot of real blood and a dead man, then pull back to establish the context and the jump in time.

Here's another example of a visual transition.

Exterior: Day - A man and a woman in a country field kissing. Followed by a sequence showing first, a heart shape, then pulling back to show a different man than we saw before pasting up a billboard which is covering the old one. The old one was a heart. It was an add for a dating service. The new billboard is an add for Cell Phones. The man putting up the billboard is thinking: "Why wasn't Mary home when I called her?"

Here we again use symbolism, in this case the icon of a heart to make the jump. But we can also do it with poses. In my graphic novel *Lex Luthor: The Unauthorized Biography*, I employed transitions involving people in similar poses when we jumped from one scene to the next to make the visual jump in a manner that was smooth. It can seem a little flashy, so you have to be careful using this technique. The effect should be subliminal. In the case of the Lex Luthor book, I often used it as a metaphor. In one scene we see the photo of a murdered man. The first shot of the next scene showed him in the same position, only lying in bed, waking up from a nasty drunk. You can play with visual transitions in many different ways

The trouble with visual transitions in comics, you have to get your artist to agree to do them. Not that they're such a big thing to ask for, but you'd be surprised how some artists feel about the writer making visual demands. And sometimes the artist will just plain forget to do them. If you're a film maker, this is less of an issue.

Textual

Example of a transition using text. In this case, a narration is the bridge. A super hero is flying over a city, looking for something. Captions read: "I spend three hours on patrol over the city. No sign of the Fish. But something tells me, he's down there..." We cut to a shot of a man in a three piece suit with a Fishhead, instead of a human head, having a meeting with his henchman in a shabby looking loft. Caption: "...somewhere." Dialog: "All right you guys. Let's talk about our next job."

In the above example we see the broken caption that begins in the last shot and ends in the first panel of the next scene. This technique has been used heavily since it was popularized by Alan Moore ("Watchmen") in the mid-eighties.

Example: Three panel scene showing two men arguing. Man 1, Panel 1: I'm telling you, she stole the rock! Man 2, panel 2: You're out of your mind! Sheila would never do that! Man 1, Panel 3: "Well, get ready for a shock, buddy. 'Cause she's been caught on video." Below this a two panel sequence. A woman has a small black box in her hand. A jewelry box. She's standing in an expensive looking office before a desk. We can't see the man on the other side because he's off panel. She holds out the box to him, smiling. Dialog: "I've brought you the rock, Dino." The next panel shows the man on the other side of the desk, taking the box from her hand, smiling: Dialog: "Nice work, baby."

The above example linked the two scenes with dialog that was about the same subject. It was a logical flow of the story from a scene discussing the theft, to a shot of the thief passing on the loot to her employer. This transition used subject as a linking device. You can also use symbolic transfers by using symbolic dialog in place of visual symbolism as in this example:

Example: Two panel scene. A man is standing over the body of a cat that has been killed. The man's really upset. Panel 1 dialog: "Kilroy!" Panel 2: "They killed you....didn't they. I know it was them." Below that a two panel sequence showing a woman sitting on a couch with an empty bottle of tequila sitting on the coffee table before her and a shot glass in her hand. She looks drunk and depressed. Panel 1: "My career's dead. It's over..." Panel two, she bends forward and cries, putting her face in her hands.

Random

Random transitions involve jumps to new scenes without any apparent linking device. However, this is misleading. The linking device is the logical progression of events. As we see in the following example, there is a reason we made the jump. It makes perfect sense.

Example: Three panels of two people fighting in a desert. In the Background are the smoking ruins of an airplane. Below that a two panel scene showing a group of military men in a command tent, looking at maps. Dialog: "They've got to be somewhere in sector seven. Send out some recon patrols.")

The transition made no sense visually, nor were there any linking words. But there was a sense of sequential storytelling at work. We made the assumption that the man in the tent was talking about the two people fighting in the first scene. The sequence seems logical and our mind puts together the story. Two men crashed in the desert and end up fighting over something. Meanwhile, a rescue party is out looking for them.

Random jumps must involve some kind of logical progression in the story. The progression need not be apparent in the first panel of the following scene, but it should be apparent in the following panel. If you confuse the Audience too much, they will be forced to go back and reread the previous page again and that will interrupt the story flow.

REMEMBER: Transitions must be clear. They keep the story moving smoothly.

FLASHBACKS

This is one of the most abused, misunderstood, and over used techniques in fiction. But, when handled properly, it can achieve powerful results.

Flashbacks are a look back in time, revealing the backstory. They should never be used at the beginning of a story and they should never dominate a story. This is because flashbacks stop the story midstream, announce that we are now going somewhere else, and jump back in time. So they must be important enough to do that. If you need to show some element of the backstory in a visual way, this is a method, but understand a few things about flashbacks first.

They are essentially a form of exposition. They exist for the express purpose of passing on information to the audience. So they need to be dynamic and entertaining on their own.

They should play as one act stories with a trigger event. The climax of the flashback should have a powerful dramatic punch. This will add to the energy of the main story.

They should be kept to a minimum, because this technique announces itself as a technique more strongly than any other. The Audience receives a jolt to their suspension of disbelief. In real life we can't play back time. Audiences are used to flashbacks, but they are a distraction if done without a good reason. And many find them annoying, because they interrupt the story flow.

One way to make flashbacks more natural is to treat them as a character's memory. Or a narration of an event the character witnessed. We show the Audience what the character saw in a visual way, but it's limited by their POV.

Framing

This variant of the flashback makes the whole story a flashback, with only the opening and ending of the story in present time. The name of the technique comes from the opening and closing of the story, known as the "frame". To maintain linkage with the present, writers often insert a panel or a page in the midst of the story to remind the Audience that they're witnessing events in the past. I used this device in my graphic novel *Sinking*.

This method is used mainly to show how the past impacts on the present. The end of the story reveals how the events of the past (the main body of the story) led to the state of affairs in the present. It's a good idea to make the end sequence surprising in some way. The film *Edward Scissorhands* employed this technique. For a more complex example, I recommend the director's cut of *Once Upon a Time In America*.

REMEMBER: Flashbacks should only be used for important reasons.

TURNING CLICHÉS

Although I'm of the opinion that all clichés must die, there is a good use for them. You can use clichés to set up the audience's expectations before surprising them with something fresh.

No one has come up with a term for this, so I call it: Turning Clichés.

The definition of a cliché is an over-used expression or idea. It's mainly something you've seen a million times before. Either a stereotype, a maxim like "a bird in the hand is worth two in the bush", or a scene that's been done to death.

Audiences are bored with clichés, which is why they are to be avoided. However, because they can see one coming a mile away, you can sometimes use a cliché to lull the Audience into a false sense of security. You can lead them to believe something is going to happen, then BAM! you hit them with a completely different result.

A classic example of this is the old monologuing Villain giving a speech to the hero before he kills him scene. The Villain has the hero tied up. He's telling him his plans to conquer the world. This gives the Hero time to escape and beat the Villain. Audiences have seen this done a million times. It's in almost every James Bond movie, for example.

In the penultimate issue of *Watchmen*, the heroes Nite Owl and Rorschach show up at the "villain" Ozymandius' fortress and try to stop him. Ozymandius beats them in a fight, then tells them his plan. Thinking they could still stop him, Nite Owl says: "When are you planning to do it?" Ozymandius calmly replies: "Do it? ...I did it thirty-five minutes ago."

When you turn a cliché, you have to make the Audience

think the cliché is going to play out like it always does. So you lead them down this path, giving them little or no indication that anything is amiss before to hit them with the punchline.

If you decide to turn clichés in a story, don't do it more than once or twice. If you use this technique too often, people will expect it, and then the trick loses steam. You also have to take into account that clichés are annoying to a lot of people. If they even get a hint of one, they may not even finish reading the story.

REMEMBER: Turn clichés at your own risk.

PACING

The ability to pace a story is one of the most important talents you can possess. There's nothing worse than a story that bogs down with boring scenes or is so frantic it's over in a flash and you feel empty. Pacing is the technique that controls the flow of the story. This is done with the fine tuning of Rhythm and Tempo. The other component of pacing is Narrative Drive.

You want the pacing of the story to reflect the mood you're trying to set. If the story is about romance, you don't want the frantic pace of an action story. If you're doing an action story, you don't want the slow pace of a psychological drama.

Pace helps define mood. Mood creates feeling. The pace of the story will have an impact on how the Audience feels when experiencing it. You want the mood to be exactly what you want it to be, so pay close attention to the following systems:

Rhythm and Tempo

Rhythm is the length of the scenes in a sequence. The length of the scenes effect the ebb and flow of the story, in addition to the polarity of those scenes. If you make the scene lengths short, you speed up the Rhythm. If you stretch them out, you can slow the rhythm down. As a rule of thumb, the act climax scenes are the longest in a story. They are where the most critical moments take place. Building toward the act climax, the scenes are usually short for reasons of tempo.

Tempo is the level of activity in a scene. If the scene involves wild action, that's a different tempo than a scene with two people sitting on a couch talking about existentialism. You want the tempo exciting when building toward an act climax. The Kinetic Principle is a rule that says the shorter the scenes, the more intense the tempo. In my first comic series, *Espers,* I employed this technique in the fourth issue. The scenes building toward the story climax were short. Sometimes one panel in length. And I added a ticking clock. This gave an intense urgency to the whole build up to the climax.

It wasn't something I'd read about back then, it was something I came up with on my own. And now you know the reason it works.

Narrative Drive

Narrative drive is the power of the story. If the story has a lot of power and momentum, it will drive the scenes and the pace will be amplified. Even if the pace is actually slow, a strong narrative drive adds more emotional energy.

You control the narrative drive with story values and scene polarity. By carefully choosing the importance of the events in a scene, you can increase or decrease the narrative drive.

IRONY

Most people see irony as the nature of the universe. Positive and negative forces cancel each other out, like matter and anti-matter. In fiction, irony is somehow amusing to us because it shows that both sides can lose a war.

Irony is also used to show improbable coincidence can happen, or that expression an intent are two different things.

In the film *The Last Emperor,* it was shown that the Emperor of China was revered as a god, lived in an incredible palace surrounded by an army of servants, but had no power and was a virtual prisoner. This is irony. That someone so powerful could be so powerless.

The film *Moulin Rouge (1952)* tells the story of the great artist Henri Toulouse-Lautrec. All through the film, he searches for someone who will love him for who is and not what he looks like, but when he finds her, he dumps her. This is irony.

The Audience believes in Newtonian laws. They like to see causality. If someone has power, we should see the pros and the cons of that power. If someone has money, we should see why that's a problem. Irony adds a sense of verisimilitude and depth. Irony also makes for good endings to stories, because it's more believable to Audiences than the perfect happy ending. There's humor in Irony that can also be exploited.

The film *Sullivan's Travels* is a great study in how irony can be used to comedic effect. Joel McCrea plays John L. Sullivan, a director who wants to make a meaningful films about human suffering. So he dresses up like a hobo and goes out on the road to learn how real people live. All his life, Sullivan's had nothing but good luck, so he doesn't know what suffering is like. But no matter where he goes good fortune smiles upon him. People take him in and give him food and clothes, beautiful women buy him meals. And even worse, when he tries to hitch a ride on a truck, it takes him back to Hollywood! Finally he decides to use his money to help the poor, so he starts handing out money to all the homeless he meets and is robbed. It gets worse from there, but I don't want to spoil this great film. One of the ironies of the film is when he looks for trouble he can't find it. When he isn't looking for it, he finds it in spades.

The first super-hero story ever written was all about irony. Philip Wylie's *The Gladiator* was about a man with superpowers who fought for our side during World War I. He was a great hero during the war, but afterward he realized there was no place for a person like him in society. People were afraid of him. After all, someone with the powers of extreme brute force are only useful for destructive purposes. They have no place in a peaceful world. So the irony was, all that power made him a hero in war and a pariah in peacetime.

REMEMBER: Irony adds a sense of realism and can make serious events funny.

THEMES

A theme is defined as a main idea or an underlying meaning of a literary work that may be stated directly or indirectly.

There are two kinds of theme in literature, a main theme and a minor one. The main theme would be that which the story is really about, like Greed is destructive, for example. A minor theme might be lust is blind. Something that goes with the main theme but has its own sub plot.

Themes are not subjects. A Subject is a topic which acts as a foundation for a story while a theme is an opinion expressed on the subject.

Themes can be related to the premise or not. They usually are. But they are never dealt with in an obvious way. They are interwoven into the fabric of the story the way the premise is.

When something happens to us, we don't vocalize what the theme or premise of that event was, because we're never seeing it that way. Neither should our fictional characters. The events in a story are carefully constructed by a writer to create the themes and the premise, but they should be a natural component of everything that happens. They can't be so obvious that the characters themselves would be aware of them.

But the characters *can* discuss the issues that affect their lives in the story we present, as if they are subconsciously understanding their role in the story.

A classic example of a major theme would be "War is Hell". This is explored in a ton of war stories and movies. The theme is explored through the dialog and the events that take place in the story. They all come together to form a gestalt. A theme can be introduced in myriad ways but you don't want to make it too obvious. It should unfold naturally. You can do it in the casual conversation two characters are having. You can do it in the descriptions of scenes to evoke a mood. You can do it with the decisions your characters make and their ramifications.

Themes give the story more resonance. They can make a generally simple story seem to have more depth and value.

When employing themes you want to create scenes that explore the theme the same way a story explores a premise. The theme becomes the premise of the scene.

You can also use themes as a form of color for the story. For example, you can explore food and cooking, or fashion, or music. This use of themes gives the story more of a light hearted feel, and provides a nice sort of resonance.

Anyway you choose to use themes can help add some depth and literary wit to your story. They're a nice technique to play with.

REMEMBER: Themes enhance the story and provide depth and resonance.

FORESHADOWING

There's a method for creating a feeling of anticipation in the audience by playing with their subconscious. It's called foreshadowing. Foreshadowing involves cuing the audience early on that something is going to happen. But you do it in a subtle manner, so they don't take notice of it on a conscious level.

There are several approaches to this technique. One is visual, the other is textual. When employing foreshadowing you don't want the audience to see what you're doing. You want them to feel it.

Shakespeare employed the textual method with dialog in *Julius Caesar*. In the beginning of the play the characters keep using terms that involve cutting, stabbing, knives, etc. This foreshadows the scene where Caesar gets assassinated. Other dialog also indicates harm to Caesar in an indirect way. For example, Caesar is walking through a crowd with Cassius, Casca and Brutus:

SOOTHSAYER: Beware the ides of March.

CAESAR: What man is that?

BRUTUS: A soothsayer bids you to beware the ides of March.

Later, Brutus talks to Casca about Caesar's epileptic fit in the throng.

CASCA: ...before he fell down, when he perceived the common herd was glad he refused the crown, he plucked me ope his doublet and offered them his throat to cut. ...Three or four wenches , where I stood, cried 'Alas, good soul!' and forgave him with all their hearts: but there's not heed to be taken of them; if Caesar had stabbed their mothers, they would have done no less.

Later still Casca talks to Cassius about Caesar:

CASCA: Indeed, they say the senators tomorrow mean

to establish Caesar as a king; and he shall wear his crown by sea and land, in every place, save here in Italy.

CASSIUS: I know where I will wear this dagger then. And so on...

The dialog serves to cue the audience that Caesar is doomed, because he is blessed with power that other's don't want him to have.

The visual foreshadowing technique can be accomplished one of two ways. Both are symbolic, but one form is more abstract. Therefore I call this first method abstract foreshadowing.

In abstract foreshadowing, you cue the reader with a symbol you prepare for them. This symbol is used when certain things happen. Every time, for example, something bad happens you show the symbol somewhere. Then, when you use the symbol later on, the audience subconsciously understands that something bad is going to happen soon. The symbol can be anything you choose. A woman wearing a big hat, a Christian fish icon, a laughing baby, a dog rooting through garbage, a smiley face button.

This technique must be done in a carefully balanced way so the audience recognizes the symbol, but isn't hit over the head with it. You want them to be cued, not to be slammed. Otherwise, the technique becomes a parody. Like the fruit cart that always gets smashed in movie car chase scenes.

The second method involves giving the audiences incomplete glimpses of the future. I call this the Oracle method. If the story takes place in the past, you can use a framing sequence to suggest something happens in the story that leads to a certain conclusion. For example, your story's narrator can have one arm, but in the main body of the story, he has two arms.

You can also have a character get incomplete glimpses of the future in dreams, visions, or it can be foreshadowed through the knowledge other characters have of things that will affect the hero that he is still ignorant of.

Both the "abstract" and "oracle" methods can also be used in text. Symbolic phraseology can be used to preceed events as we saw in Julius Caesar. Oracle methods can also be used in dialog.

REMEMBER: Foreshadowing creates anticipation subconsciously. It shouldn't be obvious.

SYMBOLISM

Another method that adds resonance to a story and helps to amplify the themes and the premise is symbolism. It creates a resonance in the mind of the Audience that helps establish mood, feeling, and emotion. It plays with our subconscious in ways that can achieve

Symbolism can be used in a variety of ways, both visually and sub-textually.

All human beings respond to symbolism. It seems to be a universal language that all people understand. Psychologists like Carl Jung have theorized that we have a collective unconscious and certain things are known to us all. Symbolism is our collective way of interpreting things. A heart is often represented as a shape that looks nothing like a real heart. The sun is usually drawn as a circle with lines coming out of it. But symbolism isn't limited to icons. We understand some things as symbolism because they evoke a feeling in us. They represent something to us. The Jack O'Lantern means Halloween to us. The Turkey means Thanksgiving. The Christmas Tree, Christmas. A rattle or pacifier translates to "baby". A man in a suit, carrying a briefcase, can mean "father" or "executive". A woman in an apron can mean "mother".

But you can create your own symbols in a story by attaching meaning to an object or sign of your choice. It doesn't have to be everyday symbols people expect.

The use of symbolism can be used to foreshadow events, as we saw in the last chapter. They can also be used as a form of commentary on the story. It can be used as a counterpoint to events in the scene. Or it can be used to amplify the message or tone of the scene.

Symbolic Charge

When symbolism is used to evoke an archetypal feeling in the work, this is known as symbolic charge. Just as symbolic characterization makes a character look like what they're supposed to be, symbolic charge uses symbolism to enhance the feel of the story so it matches an archetypal model you've chosen.

In the movie BRAZIL, papers were always in evidence, floating on a breeze or stacked to the ceiling, suggesting a bureaucracy. The use of air tubes all over the place added with sounds resembling a growling stomach gave the symbolic charge that the people lived in the bowels of some enormous creature. So the symbolic charge of this film gave you the feeling that everyone had been swallowed by a totalitarian beast.

The symbolic choices were logical to the milieu and didn't seem out of place, yet they also served to make the story resonate with a feeling which enhanced the work. It really made you feel the nightmarish quality of the world, even though you could laugh at its excesses.

Symbolism gives a writer freedom to add double levels of meanings to his work: a literal one that is self-evident and the symbolic one whose meaning is far more profound than the literal one.

REMEMBER: Symbolism works best when it's integrated into the story in a non-obtrusive way. It should work on the subconscious of the audience, not hit them over the head.

ICONS

When symbolism is boiled down to its purest, most representational form, you are left with the icon. Icons are something we're all familiar with. From the stop sign to the smiley face button, icons are a common form of communication in our post-industrial society.

They have a strong power on a psychological level

because they have immediate recognition value. People know what an icon stands for when they see it. And depending on the emotional charge that icon has for them, it can be used in powerful ways.

The American Flag is often used to promote patriotism. The cross to promote Christianity. Santa Claus to promote Christmas. If you choose a icon with the right symbolic power for what you want to say, you can pass a message onto the audience without any elaboration. If they see a preacher standing before a cross, they feel the religious resonance. And if you invert that cross and put the guy a hooded robe, they know what that means, too.

Icons are a great form of communication. But you should be careful about sending mixed messages with them. If you want to use an icon to say something different for ironic effect, you need to make it clear.

The smiley face icon with a bullet hole between the eyes is a good example of mixed message icons. It tells you, basically, that the person displaying this icon hates cheerful people.

One of the reasons icons have such a powerful charge is that simplicity is easy to understand. It allows the mind to complete the picture. Just as prose allows the mind to evoke an image of its own. When you give someone the minimum amount of information to understand a concept, their mind has the freedom to extrapolate and build on the idea. The more information you provide, the less room for thought, because you start fencing in the realm of probabilities. The receiver also has to absorb more data.

Icons provide clear cut messages. just don't use them to muddy the waters and you'll do fine.

SEMIOTICS

Semiotics is the language of the medium. Comics have their own method of passing information to the audience.

We've covered some of them already. Scott McCloud's excellent book UNDERSTANDING COMICS delves into the subject in great depth.

It's important to understand some of the conventions of the medium, because they can help you or hinder you.

One of the first conventions of Comic Book Semiotics that stick out is the sound effect. Since we don't see sounds, we hear them, this can look jarring to someone unfamiliar with comics. (And believe me, there are people very unfamiliar with them). Since comics, at this stage of the game, is a two dimensional print medium, sound has to be shown as a word floating around the space of the panel. The sound effect tells us this is the sound the characters are hearing. It's purpose is to make us experience the scene as if we were there.

Sound effects are often misused by people who think they are necessary for everything. They're not. Sound effects exists to emphasize a moment.

DIALOG

"Less is more."
Anonymous

THE NATURE OF DIALOG

If there's anything as important as the structure and the characterization, it's the dialog.

That's why it gets its own section..

People will judge you heavily by your dialog. Even if the plot is bad, the dialog can make you look good. There are a lot of half-baked stories out there people like because of the dialog. But dialog is no substitute for a great story. They should go hand in hand.

The technique of writing good dialog is fairly simple. But it can still be very tough to get right. It boils down to a few simple rules:

1. Dialog is not real conversation. It's only supposed to sound real.

2. It must sound realistic. Say it out loud to be sure.

3. Keep it short and sweet. No one likes long winded conversations except the person saying them.

4. If you've heard it before, think of another way of saying it.

5. All clichés must die!

6. Research! Cultures and sub-cultures have their own idioms and patois.

7. Dialog should not be expected unless you want it to be. In other words, surprise the Audience, don't bore them.

In literature, dialog comes in two distinct types. Inner and outer dialog. Inner is best confined to prose and comics but is extremely hard to do well in film or plays

Inner Dialog – In inner dialog, the characters speak to themselves and reveal their personalities. It's their inner thoughts. In comics, it would be shown in thought balloons or captions. To use inner dialog, writers often employ techniques like stream of consciousness or dramatic monologue. You can find such dialogs in the works of Stephen King, Frank Miller, and William Faulkner.

Outer Dialog – These are simple conversations between two characters used in almost all types of fictional works. It's the most common form that you see. Whenever two people are talking in a story, it's outer dialog.

Dialog is *not* real conversation. Real conversation is a boring and oppressive when translated to print. People use too many "Ums" and "Ahs" and "You knows" and "I means" and lots of other redundant words and sounds.

Dialog needs to be memorable. It can't be even remotely dull. Because any forgettable dialog sucks energy from your story. Good dialog adds to the pleasure of reading and thus adds energy to the story.

More importantly, whatever people say to each other in a story, it has to move the story along. It has to have a purpose. You do not want dialog that wastes time and goes nowhere. You must have had conversations with people in real life

The "show, don't tell" rule applies as much to dialog as anything else we've talked about. If you can show us something visually, instead of telling us, it will work better for you. If not, then make that dialog zing.

Dialog should first be dramatic, then informational. That is your priority. Every line should advance the story and help make the responding dialog more exciting.

Have you ever seen a conversation between two people where you were just dying to hear everything they say because each line made you want to hear the other character's response? You need to be able to do that in your story. You need to make those lines of dialog count.

This is helped by following the above rules. Now let's get into specifics.

Prolixity

This is a form of writing that must be avoided at all cost. Unless you are doing it on purpose. Prolixity is the term for sentences that use too many words. Too many words makes a sentence boring. It makes it passive.

"We talked for what seemed like days as the cold September morning turned to afternoon, then night, then morning again as we talked and talked some more about all the things that were on our minds and all the things we should have done to stop the terror that was ravaging the city while we impotently looked on. Finally, we had a plan after discussing all the possible outcomes of every action we could take to end the problems that faced us."

Aside from taking too long to say what it has to say, the above paragraph is full of redundancy. When you take too long to say something, your writing becomes vague. It causes the audience's mind to wander. Think back on those days in high school when some boring teacher droned on about history or math. Remember how you would rather be doing something else? We'll you don't want the reader to feel that way. You want them to be *excited* and *involved*. Anything but bored.

The above paragraph would read better this way:

"We talked from dawn till dusk till dawn again, covering every possible contingency. The fear that was ravaging the city had to be stopped. Now we had a plan."

Less is More

Short sentences have more punch. Long sentences take longer to read, so the energy it takes to read them is dragged out and diminished. People respond to sound bites more than to speeches. This is why people with emotionally charged causes sound more correct on television, even though they're usually presenting disinformation and/or out and out propaganda.

The human mind accepts information more easily when the information comes in simple bursts. You're driving down a highway and see a sign that says:

FOOD

This has more resonance for most people than: JOHN'S COUNTRY KITCHEN SERVING HOT MEALS AT A GOOD PRICE.

Both work, but the first one is primal. It allows you to fill in the blanks and create a immediate image in your mind. The second tells you more information and thus you have more to process in your mind. It complicates things.

If there was a sign that said: JOHN'S COUNTRY KITCHEN SPECIALIZING IN HAMBURGERS, STEAKS, BREAKFAST FOODS. WE ALSO HAVE SHAKES, MUFFINS, PIES AND OTHER CULINARY TREATS TO WHET YOUR APPETITE.

This is even more information. It's also more specific. It robs us of our imagination. A vegetarian might be put off by all the mention of meat products. A dieter might think...too fattening, move on. But a sign that says FOOD allows us to become curious and want to find out more. It only tells us what we need to know. Nothing more.

The object of prose is to keep the reader interested. To keep their eyes glued to the page. You want them to read the next sentence and the next and the next. You want to stimulate them.

Keeping the text short and sweet does this very well. It retains more mystery, which due to human nature, makes the reader curious to know more. We want to know what's in the box, what's behind that door. As a writer, you're leading them through a great castle, through secret passages, up stairs, through cavernous halls. You should keep their excitement high as they explore the mysteries you're about to unfold.

Short sentences are snappy. They are easy to read, easy to understand. When you write a line of dialog or a line of prose in a caption, take a hard look at it. See if you can't cut words, shorten it. See if it can't be said more strongly, more effectively.

REMEMBER: Less is more when it comes to prose.

TEXT AND SUBTEXT

We've already covered the difference between text and subtext. Now let's try to understand how it works for dialog.

In bad fiction, people say exactly what they mean to each other. This is also done in children's fiction, because children don't have the facility to understand subtext as well as adults. But when I say children, I mean young children.

In fact, a lack of subtext marks any story as shallow. Subtext adds dimension to the work and adds meaning to the dialog.

The most effective way to engage an Audience is to give their minds something to work with. It isn't enough to show them things. You also want to *hint* at things. When the mind receives incomplete information, it tries to fill in the blanks. Subtext creates more depth for the Audience and it causes them to feel the hidden meaning behind the words.

Example A man and a woman are facing each other across the dinner table. The man says: "Did you do anything interesting today?" His expression is somewhat challenging and suspicious. The woman won't meet his eyes, but she has a slight smirk: "Oh, nothing. I just saw an old friend."

The emotions revealed on a character's face colors the meaning of the words. We don't have the benefit of sound in comics or prose, so we can't deal with inflection and word stress without using artificial semiotics. Actors can do that on film. But with emotional expressions, the subtext of the conversation is revealed. The man doesn't trust the woman. He feels she's cheating on him. The woman is feeding his jealousy, taunting him with vague answers. She may very well be cheating on him. In prose you can give us a sense of what is happening in the description but also in the subtext of the words.

Example: Same dialog, same couple, same setting, but their expressions are friendly and smiling.

Notice how the subtext changes in this new example. Suddenly, they seem interested in each other and now it looks like this is all part of some kind of courting ritual. It seems innocent and straightforward. But you could have the same happy expressions but you could word the dialog in such a way as to add the same sub text the expressions did previously, You can play with sub text a whole lot of ways.

Subtext changes the meaning of a scene, so the actions of the characters when they talk must be carefully selected. The choice of words is also critical. Some words can be used to suggest the subtext more strongly, creating a level of irony.

REMEMBER: Never forget to use subtext in a conversation.

EXPOSITION

"Plot exposition that can be gently wound out by the authorial voice and internal monologue of a character in the length of a page has to be delivered in a matter of seconds on the stage."

Terry Pratchett

This is the term used for dialog that reveals information to the audience. In bad fiction, this is usually the worst kind of dialog. That's because it's the hardest dialog to write convincingly. Unfortunately, it's almost impossible to write a story without expositional dialog. So let's try to understand how to make it work.

As we've discussed earlier, dialog is not real conversation, but it must *seem* real. The primary goal of dialog is to create drama, the secondary goal is to impart information. It's important to keep these priorities straight. Too many writers try to cram tons on information into a word balloon without first considering whether it would be something a person would say. Or even more importantly, what this dialog does for the story dramatically.

You probably remember some teacher back in school who was a complete bore when he gave lectures. Information cannot be merely told to someone. It needs to be imparted in a dynamic, interesting manner. It's extremely easy to bore someone if you're not careful.

Public speaking classes teach you to make your points in short, sharp sentences with sufficient breaks between them so the audience can absorb what they heard. The same rule applies to writing. You have to convert your exposition into ammunition. The dialog has to sing with emotional meaning. It can't just be raw data. It needs to have an impact on the character who's receiving it.

If the dialog has no value in the scene, it will have no value to the reader. So it's a bad idea to waste their time with meaning less chatter. Each line of dialog should further the story, define the characters, create emotion, add humor, or provide information. If it fails to do any of these things, consider dumping it.

So, when writing expositional scenes, you want to avoid table dusting. You want to make the passing of information to the audience seem as natural as a blue sky. To do this you have to carefully choose who says what to whom. The person receiving the information should not be aware of it, unless they are playing the fool for some reason. The person giving the information should only tell the other character the bare minimum of what they should know. As we discussed before, it's boring to hear too much too soon. Tell us only what we *need* to know. Show us the rest whenever possible.

It's much better for the story if the information passed on has some kind of emotional impact on the other character. Either it makes them laugh, cry, scared, or angry. If it's boring to the receiver, don't expect the audience to be too interested either.

When you create emotional meaning out of the dialog, you add to the energy of the scene and you advance the story.

Let's explore some examples of expositional dialog to see how we can approach it differently.

Art Insert: A man and woman talking in what looks like a business meeting in an office.

MAN: I remember Kyle telling me about Lancaster. He said Lanc had some business dealings with Arabs.

WOMAN: I happen to know he has connections to several high ranking members of the Saudi Royal Family.

MAN: Then...you think this is about the sword?

WOMAN: Definitely.

In the above example, the two characters are talking about someone they both know. Notice the man has incomplete data and the woman seems to know more. She tells him what he needs to know in an indirect way. This is realistic behavior and it doesn't seem forced.

In the next example we look at a case where someone's boss is providing info to an employee. This is basically a lecture, but watch how it's done...

EXAMPLE: A mob boss is talking to a soldier. They're in a warehouse full of crates. Hiding behind one of the crates, listening in, is Kyle.)

BOSS: Vic...the shipment comes in at three A.M. sharp. I don't expect any trouble. But you and Carlos better keep an eye out, capiche?

VIC: You expect Kyle?

BOSS: Don't worry about that milk sucking freak. I've taken care of him.

From this discussion, information is passed, but we only get the information absolutely necessary. And there are implied elements in the dialog that suggests Kyle is a threat, that this shipment is illegal or something others will want in on. All of this is done with subtext. You only say what you need to say, and try to be indirect about it so the reader has something to imagine. When you spark the audience's imagination, you give them something to anticipate. You provide an element of mystery.

In the following example, we find out about a third character through dialog between two people.

Example: Two soldiers are sitting in a trench during some war. They're passing the time, talking.)

239

BOB: What up, Cort? Where's Pete? I've been looking for him.

CORT: Didn't you hear? He stepped on a land mine. Blew his friggin' legs off.

BOB: Jesus! When did that happen?

CORT: Last week. They sent him home already.

BOB: Home!? The bastard owes me two hundred bucks! How am I ever going to get it back?

In the above example we find out that Bob is owed money by Pete. And the subtext is, Bob cares more about the money than about Pete's misfortune. This defines Bob's character and suggests he may have a pressing reason for wanting that money back.

Exposition should tell us things the way a fly on the wall would hear it. When people who know each other are talking, they use a shorthand because they both have common knowledge and they're not going to repeat information to each other they already know. So you need to set up the conversation so the audience can understand what they're saying by what's *not* said. This adds more realism to the dialog.

As an exercise, go to a bar or a restaurant at a busy time and eavesdrop on other people's conversations. Study how they pass information back and forth. There are specific ways people talk to each other based on the nature of the conversation. Mating rituals are different than business transactions (most of the time, anyway). Study the differences and try to discern the relationships of the people based on the way they communicate with each other.

REMEMBER: Convert your exposition to ammunition.

STYLIZED DIALOG

One of the goals of writing dialog is to make each character sound like a unique individual. People don't all sound alike. But we can't deal with the actual pitch of a person's voice in comics. We can't do inflection and intonation without resorting to artificial tricks.

So that leaves stylized dialog.

This method helps create a unique voice for each character and provide yet another dimension to their persona. When stylized dialog is done well, people will think you write great dialog. Quentin Tarantino made a big name for himself with his dialog in movies like *Reservoir Dogs* and *Pulp Fiction*. He kept it funny, fresh and unpredictable. On the other hand, you can make a bad name for yourself if you don't handle stylized dialog well.

There are two forms to this technique. One is speech patterns, the other is lingo. People from certain sub-cultures or ethnicities have distinctive ways of talking that set them apart from others. The contrast in their speech patterns can make them stand out as characters, but you must be careful not to make their dialog sound dated.

"Wow, man. That cat's really groovy. Dig that beat, daddyo!"

Dialog like that dates the work. We're talking 1950s, early 60s beatnik culture. You have to be careful when using slang. When you choose the style of a character's dialog, be aware of what period it dates them as being from. An old hippy in the 1990s might still retain certain speech patterns from his youth, like the use for the word "man" at the end of sentences. Someone who was young in the 1940s may still retain some 1940s style speech patterns. But most people grow up.

SLANG AND PATOIS

The late, great writer Elmore Leonard said: "Use regional dialect, patois, sparingly."

His reason: Once you commit to it for a character, then you have to use it every time that character talks and that can get tiresome for the writer and in many cases, the audience.

It's very effective when you want to make a character sound different, but it has to be convincing. Fake accents and slang no one really uses anymore can throw people out of the moment you created for them. People will go along with your story and if something seems off, you can start to lose them.

Regional dialects can work well for you if done correctly, but remember that it can also be a burden, unless it's mainly used by minor characters.

Slang can make a book seem really hip if it's up-to-date and contemporary. But the problem with slang is most of it becomes dated in two or three years.

In America slang comes mainly from our sub-cultures. Computer hackers have their own slang, surfers have theirs, etc. The black population arguably produces the most slang in the American vernacular. Since the late 80s, early 90s, hip hop slang became the parlance of the youth culture, which is similar to the beat generation's adoption of jazzbo slang in the thirties through fifties.

The problem with slang is it can seem really forced if not used properly. Having a character from a subculture talk in slang all the time sounds phony. Most people intersperse slang in their dialog. They don't use it in every sentence. Don't be fooled by pop songs and rap music. That isn't the way people actually talk. Music is a distillation of feeling. Dialog is something else all together. It has to sound real.

Slang needs to be used to make points. It shouldn't be over used. The rule for slang is the same for exposition. Convert your slang to ammunition. Make it have an impact. Use it sparingly. Don't wear it out.

If you're writing street characters, it may be wiser to use universal slang that has stood the test of time. That way, people who read your comic ten years in the future won't laugh at it. You want your work to stay in print forever, if possible.

PROFANITY

The late great comic writer and editor Archie Goodwin once had this to say: "A little profanity goes a long way."

The rules for profanity are the same for slang and exposition. You don't want to over use it. Profanity can have a strong impact in a story is used sparingly. It can really highly a character's emotional state.

When profanity is used all the time in a story, most people are turned off. The public is more forgiving of profanity today than ever before, but there are still a lot of people who don't like it. Ask yourself if you want to lose readers or audience members. You have to be aware of the limitations of the words.

Yes, profanity is used all the time in real life. Some people fill their conversations with it. But it has the effect of making people look uncouth. Consider that when you use it.

Profanity comes in degrees of offensiveness. You can easily get away with "damn" and "hell", because few people are offended by those words anymore. But racial epithets and some of the extreme four letter words and their variations are dangerous territory. You have to think carefully when using them. It can seriously limit your audience.

When words offend the audience, it can make them stop liking your story. It can ruin the spell that your story was weaving around them. Think about who your target audience is. Decide if you want to risk alienating them.

You're the master of your story and also the first editor of what your characters say. So consider these points when you decide to have someone curse.

Let's look at the categories so we can filter them out:

Profane Words

These are words that use terms religions have considered sacred. In the Judeo-Christian tradition, this primarily means taking the Lord's name in vain (that is, not in prayer).

"Good God, stop it."

"Jesus Christ, that's a big one!"

Curse Words

A *curse* calls upon a deity, or fate, to visit harm on someone or something.

Mild curse: Damn this thing!

Strong curse: Goddamn that woman!

Go to hell!

A lighter curse would be: I'll be damned.

Swearing

Swearing is to take an oath, as if to say you will be punished if you break it. At least, that's the implication.

"I swear, I didn't mean it!"

"By God, I will do my best."

Obscenities

This often refers to sexual insults or statements. It can also be scatological.

"My dick is hard."

"This shit is real."

REMEMBER: Profanity has power, but that same power can turn people away.

NARRATION

"Let me tell you a story."

This is the oldest form of storytelling. We still use the technique of a narrator filling us in on what happened. Often, this is told by either an unrelated person or someone who was witness to the events.

When you have one central character telling a story, it's common to write it from first person, with the central character playing the narrator. The central character is not always the hero in these stories. Sometimes they are only telling the story of the hero, as they see it.

The rules of exposition apply equally to narration, if not moreso. Narration tells the audience what's happening in the story, but it needs to serve a dramatic function as well as an informational one. You don't want the narrating character to be as boring as a math professor. Always remember you are trying to entertain the audience. That has to be foremost in your mind at all times.

But there's a hitch to doing narration. You don't want it to draw too much attention to itself. The narration serves to lead us into the key scenes of the story. That's what its job is. It also opens up the story at the beginning and closes it at the end. But the true story is told through the scenes that are played out. All the narration does is give us context.

Many a writer has made the mistake of having the narration tell us something rather banal, as if it was important. Nothing should be said that isn't illuminating or interesting. You also don't want to tells us things point blank. "This is my brother, Joe. He's the smart one in the family."

Narration should be told with style. It needs to reflect the personality of the narrator. It needs to possess an interesting "voice". Every character has their own voice. Their own way of talking. It reflects their background, ideology, world view and attitude. When you choose a character to narrate a story, they should be entertaining, without being distracting. The point of narration is to provide an over view of the story, information we need to understand the context of things. But since every story presents a point of view, when you use a narrator, keep in mind that the narrator is looking at it from a certain perspective. If you use an impersonal, god-like narrator, who isn't in the story, then it can just be straight information. In which case it should be concise.

The movie *Blade Runner* originally didn't have a narrator. And it works without it but the studios felt it needed one. Harrison Ford narrates the film but he sounds slightly unhappy about it, like they made him do it. Sometimes narration isn't needed but when you're dealing with a complex subject or world, it helps to explain things quickly.

Like a lot of techniques in this book, you have to choose wisely when you employ it. It has a lot of worth but it also reminds people they are listening to someone else's story and you may want them to forget that.

EXPOSITION AND INFO DUMPS

Exposition is a literary device used to introduce background information about people, places, events and so on. It is a necessary evil because without it the audience would not know what is going on. But it is also one of the most common areas people fall down on their storytelling job because they make it obvious that it's being shoved down your throat.

It should always flow naturally and unforced in the story. The methods commonly used to deliver it is a narrator's voice, character dialog or a character's thoughts. It's also given in media displays like newspaper, reports, TV newscasts, etc. Delivering exposition will be a challenge that you want to get right. You need to tell people things but you don't want to make it obvious that you're trying to educate them.

One of the worst types of exposition sounds something like this:

"So, John. Since you're my brother you known that we've been holding this family secret for a long time."

Characters who already know each other and share information do not talk that way. It sounds forced. A better way is to make the Audience wonder what they are talking about.

"John..."

"What?"

"I need to talk to you."

"Is it important, Kyle?"

"Yeah, it's about..." Kyle looks at a ring on John's hand, and nods.

"We can't talk about that. Are you crazy?"

This makes us wonder what the secret is. The word secret isn't mentioned but it's implied.

It often comes to pass that you need to prepare the reader for something that is going to happen later, as we discussed in "Set ups and Payoffs". But sometimes, we can't do it visually or we don't want to do it visually. We want to place *seeds of information* in the mind of the reader so they are prepped for an upcoming scene where we hit them with both barrels.

This technique is called leaking information. It's done by using key words in the dialog that tells the reader nothing specific, but suggests something to them. Either consciously or unconsciously. When the key words come up again, you use them in relation to more information and suddenly, they start putting pieces together. When you do this, make them work a little, it makes them feel they are discovering something important. And they love that. People do not like being fed like a goose. They like being teased and led to a mystery.

Info Dumps

I often get asked in my writing seminars how do you handle info dumps. That is those things where you need to tell a lot of info to the Audience in one fell swoop. I always say the same thing.

"Don't do it."

You don't need to use info dumps. They are clumsy and boring ways to get info to an Audience. The best way is by leaking info as discussed above. Only tell them what they need to know at that point. Nothing more. They have a lot to take in already if you are keeping them entertained. You really want to inform them without them knowing it. You want them to think they learned it themselves in the story. Obviously, you told them everything but it needs to feel like they leaned it on their own. And you do that by feeding them nibbles of information. You do that by characters having natural conversations but things are said in those conversations make the Audience wonder what they're referring to. And then you tease them with a little info so they put it together. In other words, you are leading them by the hand, gently, but in a way where they feel in control.

That is an art form and some people do it a lot better than others but you get good at it by thinking in advance how you want to tackle it . Then you work and work on the words till they sound right.

REMEMBER: Be a tease, don't be a bore.

THE WRITING PROCESS

"There's nothing to writing. All you have to do is sit at your typewriter and bleed."
Ernest Hemingway

RULES TO LIVE BY

1. A STORY IS ABOUT LIFE. LIFE MEANS CHANGE.

No story is interesting if nothing happens to the character. That goes without saying. But one way the audience knows things have occurred is when there is a net change between the beginning and end of the story. If the main character comes out ahead or behind of where he was when he started, then we know there was some kind of result to the story. A good story has some kind of result ending. Because people expect a story to have some kind of resolution.

2. YOUR STORY PREMISE IS AN ARGUMENT. PROVE IT.

All good stories have some kind of point of view. They are actually making some kind of argument about why what the main character is right or wrong. Everything that happens in that story should reinforce the argument being made (drugs are bad, kindness is good, etc.). If your story has no point of view, then it will feel directionless and pointless.

3. ALL CLICHÉS MUST DIE!

Cliches are boring. We have seen them a zillion times and they make a story feel tired. Bad dialog is often bad because it is a cliché. Anything you have seen before somewhere other than real life should not make it into your work. If someone else has used it before, then you can be sure someone else has used it also, and so on. Don't perpetuate the horror. No more Casablanca or Wizard of Oz lines. Please.

4. POLITICAL CORRECTNESS IS WRONG.

No one likes political correctness. It's dishonest. It

classifies people into artificial categories and sets them apart in some way. This is a patronizing and subtly discriminatory thing. It is not what it proposes to be. And on top of that, using PC terms dates the work, because anything so criticized and hated will become a joke in time. Already anti-PC comedies are all over the place. Using PC concepts and language will become as silly as "Jive Turkey" sooner or later. On top of that it's lame. So why do it?

5. GOOD FICTION IS 40% WRITING, 60% REWRITING.

Your first impulses are not always the best ones. We tend to regurgitate ideas before realizing later they came from some movie we saw years ago. And first draft dialog is rarely great. Because dialog is about the interaction between different people. Different characters should sound like individuals. They should have unique ideas and voices. But in the course of writing a first draft characters often sound more like the writer. So you need to tweak things and fix plot holes or weak scenes. That's why rewriting is essential to a good script.

6. STRONG STRUCTURES MAKE STRONG STORIES.

A "solid story" is a story that feels like it isn't full of holes. That is resonates with thought and complexity. The only way you can get that feeling is if the story has a good structure. If your story is just slapped together with ideas that just popped into your head, it will have lots of weaknesses and the reader will feel it.

7. SHOW, DON'T TELL.

Too many writers have characters explain things, instead of showing it. When you show something it has more impact. How many bad lectures or boring conversations have you had to endure in life? Imagine how your reader will feel listening to one of your characters droning on about plot points that happened in a previous issue. Comics are a visual medium and it works best when you can see something rather than having to read about it. Wordy descriptions should be left to prose.

8. NEVER TAKE THE CLIMAX AWAY FROM YOUR PROTAGONIST.

Also known as "Deus Ex Machina" which translates as "God from a Machine". The Ancient Greeks learned the hard way that getting your heroes out of a jam by having a miracle, like the Gods showing up at the last minute to fix things, robs the hero of their purpose and makes the story silly. It's not something you should ever do unless it serves the story, like in the end of Raiders of the Lost Ark.

9. EVERY SCENE MUST ADVANCE THE STORY.

Stories that have scenes that have no purpose in the story except to show something the writer thinks as cool or funny is a wasted scene. Because anything that doesn't serve the story in someway is interrupting the flow of the story. A story should build and move in a forward direction, so every scene should serve that purpose.

10. RESEARCH IS THE CURE FOR CLICHÉS.

The reason some things seem fresher than other things is because the writer was injecting something new and original into the mix. The best place to find ideas you haven't seen before is research. The world is a wacky, wonderful place and new things happen all the time. You should keep reading non fiction and news all the time and studying the subject matter you're dealing with to find situations and ideas that will make your work seem real. Relying purely on your own brilliance is a sure way to run out of fresh ideas.

11. NEVER TRUST YOUR FIRST IDEA. MAKE IDEA LISTS.

This goes hand in hand with the previous point. If you are writing a scene, you want it to strike people as fresh and original. So you don't want to have the first thing that comes into your head happening. That would be too easy. You should jot down everything you can think of that could happen in that scene, even thrown in ridiculous ideas. Then look them over and see which one works best. You'll be surprised what cool stuff comes out of that process.

12. IF YOU DON'T MAKE THE AUDIENCE FEEL, YOU'VE FAILED.

A story needs to make the reader feel something. Anything. I'm sure you've read many a story that you forgot about the second you put it down. Do you want your story to have that kind of effect on someone? So how do you make people feel something? Well, to start, you need to find emotional hooks to sink into the reader. You need to touch on subject or situations that are sure to get to people in one way or another. Search your own feelings about things and then work it out in the story. But try to keep shock value to a minimum as that can get old fast and it tends to cheapen things.

13. DON'T PREACH, CONVINCE.

Nothing is more boring than being preached at. No one likes having ideas shoved down their throat unless they are some kind of zealot who wants to be stoked up on whatever dogma agrees with them. In real life there are two sides to every story, sometimes more. And a story that works is a story that gives a fair shake to the different sides. You need to convince your audience that you are telling them the truth. And you won't do it by only presenting one side and making the other side look like cartoons. Most people have an innate sense of fairness, and they'll be able to tell when you are not being fair. That can go against you.

14. NEVER WRITE "ON THE NOSE." SUBTEXT ADDS DIMENSION.

Writing on the nose is an old Hollywood term. It means writing dialog that's as unsubtle as a punch in the nose. In real life, people rarely say what they really think. Therefore, your characters shouldn't either. When people talk to others, they are revealing how they feel about that person. If they suck up to someone they think they are more important. If they talk down to someone they don't respect them. And so on. You inform the reader how one character relates to the other by the way they talk to them. And rarely, ever so rarely, do they say what they really think in those conversations. But you can always get a lot of information from the context and the style of the conversation. People can understand context it's always much cooler to see than the obvious.

15. SAVE THE BEST FOR LAST.

You don't want to do all your best ideas in the beginning of a story, because then it's all downhill. Stories should be like roller coaster rides. They should have a long build to the top, then a steep scary drop, then some twists and turns and then go to another rise before hitting you with the best part. Don't blow all your best stuff right away because you will raise people expectations and they will be let down when they get to the end.

16. TRUE CHARACTER IS REVEALED UNDER PRESSURE. ADD PRESSURE!

In real life, as it should in fiction, the true character of a person is revealed when they are put under pressure. That is when they let their guards down and show what they are made of. By applying pressure to a character we see what kind of person they are. Are they cowardly? Heroic? Mean? Altruistic? Talented? Inept? What are they? The best way to show that is showing what choices they would make in any given situation. Character is action. You define people by how they act and react to things.

17. THE END OF THE STORY SHOULD NEVER BE TELEGRAPHED.

If you were going to hit someone, would you do it in slow motion so they knew it was coming? If you were going to surprise someone, would you tell them what you were going to do ahead of time? Well then you should seriously consider how you lead up to the ending of your story, because the audience should not see it coming in advance. If they know what's going to happen, why stick around to see the end of the story? The end of a story has major importance to the reader. This goes back to rule #2. When someone reads a story or sees a movie, they walk away with the ending as their last impression. And if that impression was dull, it colors their view of the work. So don't disappoint them.

18. TAKE YOUR HERO THROUGH ALL STORY VALUES.

There's a whole chapter dealing with story values. If you are unsure what they are skip to that chapter. But basically, in order to show things have happened for your character you need to show that they have been through the extremes of human experience. Happiness to sorrow. Riches to rags. Hate to love. And so on. If the character does not go through the appropriate extremes in your story, then the story does not have much emotional range and you will probably fail to move people.

19. RESPECT THE AUDIENCE.

You're expecting people to spend money on your product. You expect them to come back for more. Do you really think they will want to if you don't treat them right? Do you go back to restaurants with lousy food and bad service? Do you go back to stores where the clerks treat you like a moron and talk down to you? Well, it's a really bad idea to talk down to your readers, or assume that they are too stupid to understand something simple. It's also not a good plan to deliver the goods in a haphazard way, or be lay about how much effort you put into it. I don't like getting hot food served half cold. I imagine you don't either. Well, put yourself in the reader's shoes. They are not spending money expecting to get some half baked sludge. Nor do they want to wait three years to read the next chapter. You have to make an effort to deliver the goods as you would expect from someone else.

20. KNOW YOUR WORLD INSIDE AND OUT.

Whether you are writing about "reality" or "fantasy" your story is set in a world of your devising. It is based on your personal interpretation of the world around you and how you see things. And since you're are creating a world, it stands to figure that it should feel like a real one to the reader. They should believe in it as much as they do the one they live in. If they don't believe in your world, then they will not find it very interesting. And if you should a lack of thought or depth in the world you created, they will not feel very inspired to pay much attention to it. It will become a dull background to a dull story. Because readers are more involved when they feel a part of the story. And that only happens when that world is real for them. Therefore, you need to understand the rules of your world and how it works well before you write about it. If someone asks you a question about how your character pays the rent, or what kind of parents they had, or why is the dragon green instead of red, you better know the answer.

21. NEVER SECOND GUESS THE AUDIENCE'S TASTES. ALWAYS WRITE FOR YOURSELF.

As some of the previous rules explained it, you need to respect the audience, you need to know the world inside and out, you need to know what the story is about, etc. The only way you can fully do that is if you love the story and the characters. You need to write something that you care about, that you believe in. If you don't, the readers will feel it, and then they will respond accordingly. You might say that a lot of mindless crap sells well and the creators probably didn't care about it. But how much of that crap is remembered years later in a positive way? The work that stands the test of time is work that is a labor of love. So don't write what you think people want to read, whether you care or not. Write what has meaning for you. Because you are human and your humanity and feelings should be reflected in the work. It is bound to affect people if you do.

22. WORRY ABOUT YOUR OWN CAREER, NOT OTHERS.

If you become a professional comics creator, it's very easy to fall into the jealousy trap that so many people are stuck in. That being the constant attention people pay to other people's popularity or success and feeling upset about it. It's easy to be annoyed when you work hard to do something you really care about while someone else makes tons of money doing their comic and they don't show enough interest in it to turn it out on a regular schedule, or to see someone else who can't even write or draw get all the attention from the fan press as a "hot talent". But you really shouldn't waste your time thinking about such things. Someone else's success is not a reflection on your talent or abilities. It merely means at that point of time and place they are successful, for whatever reason. You may have you shot at the spotlight later. But if you spend too much time getting angry about other people's success and bad mouthing them, people will only see you as jealous and spiteful, which will do you no good in the end. It's better to stay positive and focused on your own work and career. You will be much better served if you do.

23. WHEN YOUR WORK SPEAKS FOR ITSELF, DON'T INTERRUPT.

Don't explain the mystery. If you manage to thrill people and entertain them, be happy with that. I personally find it distasteful when all these behind the scenes documentaries on films are made. George Lucas being one of the worst offenders. By explaining everything away as gimmicks and tricks you do your story and your characters a disservice. I'm explaining how things are done in this book only for your edification as a fellow writer. But the magic that you put into your work should remain a mystery to all but yourself.

24. DO NOT WASTE PEOPLE'S TIME!

Even if your story is really taking up sometimes time in reality, they should never ever think that it is. They should want more, not less. So dragging out things and padding them to lengthen scenes or novels is wrong. Movies and TV shows that spend a lot of story space on pointless exercises and drama are going to bore people. And boredom is death for a writer. Do not bore!

25. GOOD WRITERS ARE NOT AFRAID TO BE HONEST WITH THEMSELVES

To write a story that has impact, you have to reveal a truth. A lot of truth is revealed through painful self reflection. You shouldn't be a afraid to express personal pain in your story as a catharsis.

STARTING OUT

When you plan to write a story, you first need to understand what A>B<C stands for.

Who is the story about?

What do they want?

Why can't they get it?

Who stands in the way?

Did you create a logline? If not do that (explained in the next chapter).

Now you have a starting point. Your next step is to figure how the best approach. What are the key things you want to have occur in the story? What kind of conflicts are involved and how do they effect the main characters?

A lot of the time, writers begin with a rough idea before they know who the characters are going to be. Like, a man is standing on the ledge of a building's 20th floor, looking down at the street below, contemplating suicide. Where do you go from there?

It's a good idea when you start with the germ of an idea, to flesh out the basic characters. Come up with personas and back stories and you just might gain insights as to where to take things.

I also recommend creating a beat sheet. This is a Hollywood concept that works well with all writing projects. It's explained after the logline chapter. I seriously recommend you do these two things when formulating your story. Create a log line and a beat sheet. It will make your life so much easier down the road. Trust me.

It's always a good idea to work out the A>B<C formula early in your story construction. Once you know what the hero's goal is, you have a clear idea what direction the story needs to go. But you shouldn't limit yourself to the first couple ideas that come to mind. It's always a good

idea to write every idea you think of down on a piece of paper. All the things you think should happen in the story.

Then ask yourself, what does the audience need to know in this story? What kind of information is crucial to making the story work?

The writing process is personal to each writer. Everyone builds their stories in their own way. Some people start with an ending, some with a scene, some with a character, and work from there.

But really, you need to know the answers to the basic questions above and build on it.

LOGLINES

I'm going to frustrate you now by telling you the most important thing you should doing the beginning that's also very simple. That's creating your logline.

Loglines are one or two sentences that describe your story. That means, if you have a movie or a novel, how would you explain it in one or two sentences. Creating the logline is not easy at all. It will drive you crazy if you have to do it after the fact. This is why it's best you figure out your logline before you write your story. It will simplify your work and make your job a lot easier.

Why is it so important? A logline is a perfect test for whether you figured out your story or not. If you can't explain it in one or two sentences you've got problems. It really should be that simple.

Example: This is a popular comedy that came out a few years back. The title of the movie alone tells you want it's about. *The Forty Year Old Virgin.* IMDB.com (The Internet Movie Database) describes it thusly: "Goaded by his buddies, a nerdy guy who's never "done the deed" only finds the pressure mounting when he meets a single mother."

See, that wasn't too hard. Except this little sentence tells you a lot. The title tells you it's about a man who never grew up. And the logline tells you, he has to lose his virginity on a dare, but he's faced with a challenge he didn't expect, winning over a woman who has kids. Kids represent responsibility and adulthood. Here we have a story about someone who has avoided something most people get out of the way early into their adulthood, but he also has to deal with the other part of that decision. What this description does is make us see the problems and the conflicts he faces. And you can see how he will be made uncomfortable which is where the humor comes in. The simplicity of this idea, the clarity of this logline, the genius of the title helped make it a very successful film.

You need to do a logline if you want to be able to sell your story, because if you try to pitch it to an publisher or sell it as a book or movie, you will need to sell it with the least amount of words. People's attention spans don't last long. You need to catch them with something that explains it as simply as possible, but also makes them see it in their mind, and hopefully, inspires them to think about it and ask questions.

When you write a logline you have to ask yourself what is it about? You'd be surprised how many writers are flummoxed by that question. A lot of people have come to me over the years and want me to read their scripts, When I ask what is it about and they have trouble telling me. They expect me to read it and find out. But here's a hard fact you need to understand. If you expect anyone to give up their time or money for your story, you better be prepared to tell them what it's about so they want to read it. Like it or not, people will not want to take time time unless they are intrigued. You will not sell a book or a movie if you can't first give us an interesting pitch in one or two sentences.

I wrote a comics series called *Blue Cat (available on Acesweekly.co.uk)* and came up with this pitch to describe it: "A teen-aged girl and her dead cat solve supernatural mysteries." What that logline does is tell you who is the hero, what are they trying to do. The dead cat part throws a curve ball at you. You want to know why and how a dead cat figures into it. And supernatural mysteries is the conflict. Solving mysteries is hard. Supernatural mysteries? Has to be a lot harder.

Your logline should tell you who it's about, what the

conflict is and to really make it work, the conflict should be something that's clashing big time with the protagonist. In the case of Blue Cat, it's the heroine, Cindy Sparks, who's a normal girl dealing with unnatural situations. The fact that they are supernatural makes you wonder what they are.

The other thing you really need, if you can fit it in, because this is what will help sell it. You need the sizzle. You need something that makes people want to find out what happens. If you can do that, you created a good logline. And having the talent to do that will serve you well..

Loglines will help you keep in mind what your main goals are. And that's important because you should know that more than anyone else.

BEAT SHEET

Aside from the log line one of the most important things you can do as a writer is break down your story into beats. The beat sheet is an idea developed in Hollywood but is immensely helpful when you write any kind of project from stories to novels, comics or screen plays. Basically it is a simple list that breaks down key events in your story. Or beats.

When I was doing monthly comics scripts, I would start typing out the numbers of pages and a paragraph that defined what was going to happen on them. When I had all the pages worked out I would take that sheet and break down my script into more detailed panel and dialog descriptions.

It's always good to know where you are going. You can always make changes. But the beauty of the beat sheet is, by mapping out the story beats, you understand the flow. And you can see what areas need work and how you can improve on your first ideas. It's never a good idea to just go with the first idea that pops in your head. But you can do it in a beat sheet and than revise it as you see everything on context.

The late Blake Snyder wrote an excellent book called *Save the Cat* which gets into log lines and Beat Sheets. I want take his standard breakdown of a beat sheet to explain how it works for a screenplay. But this method works great for everything. Not all factors apply in every case. These are the things that happen in sequence. You decide where they happen but this is their usual order. He likes to use puns to describe some of his events. You can call them whatever you want but they have to take place in the proper sequence to make sense.

Opening Image: How does the story start? What's the first thing we see?

Theme Stated: What theme are we using and how is it expressed? Usually a character other than the hero asks a question or makes a statement that is really stating the theme,

The Set Up: What is the first thing that sets up the trigger event

The Catalyst: What is the thing that sets the trigger event in motion?

The Debate: This is the discussion the hero has with others on what's the best course of action to take, They have to make up their mind but they may need convincing or they may need to convince someone.

Break into II: We enter the second act how?

B Story: What is the sub plot? This is often the love story where two characters find each other or their relationship heats up

Fun and Games: The rising action and complications start happening here. Things get real.

Midpoint: What happens in the middle of the story? Things usually get better or worse here and shift to a new level as a result

Bad Guys Close In: Now pressure is coming down on our heroes even after they might have just won a reprieve, Things start to turn.

All is Lost: This the part of the story where we are reaching the crisis point and things look like a do or die situation. This is where you usually kill off a side character like a mentor or a partner.

Dark Night of the Soul: So your hero lost someone or some thing they needed and now has to figure out what to do. This is where they are having a rough time and might want to give up. It's the crisis point.

Break into Three: The third act. A solution is figured out but will it work? The hero has to try it or they will lose everything. This is the climax.

Finale: How does your story end?

Final Image: What is the last thing we see when the story ends?

You can make a sheet or a couple sheets and write down what happens in each of these beats. When you're done you have a beat sheet and will find working from that point on a lot easier.

My advice is to take a day or two off and then return to look at it and see how you could refine and improve it. You will find fresh insight when you work it out.

This may sound like Hollywood crap to you, but it's a very sound principal and you don't have to use this exact structure. For a classic story, it happens to be a very solid approach.

AFTERWORD

"I hate writing, I love having written."
Dorthy Parker

So you want to be a writer. We discussed what that means. We discussed what it takes to make a story good. Now it's up to you.

A few things I should mention before you go on to create that masterpiece. As hard as writing something can be, it's not the hardest part. Promoting your work and yourself will be a full time job. Even if you have a publisher, you still got to let people know your work exists. You have to let them know you exist. And you have to get them to care.

It sounds like a tall order and it is. Some people are better at it than others. But before you have to worry about that you first have to produce something.

Producing work is your primary goal as a creative person. Not self promotion. Without the work you will have no career.

Even if your work fails to make you rich at first, you should never give up. The act of creation itself is its own reward. But while that won't put food on the table, you need to remember something. Sometimes it takes a long time for work to be discovered. Creating more work increases your chances of people discovering it by creating more things for people to follow. If someone likes one thing of yours, they may look for other projects you made and thus, you help build a fan base.

Never enter into this business expecting wealth. Only a select few ever get it. A real writer does it because they have to. They are driven to create. Some of the great artists of history died in poverty but their work has lived through the ages. They weren't in it for a buck.

You'll never know how successful you'll be until you try. You can't win the lottery unless you buy a ticket. Many people try and fail. Some writers don't see great success until after they're dead, like Robert E Howard, creator of Conan the Barbarian. But if he hadn't created those stories, he would have never been a huge influence on fantasy literature. Or H.P. Lovecraft who's work continues to inspire and terrify fans long decades after he passed.

Hopefully, you won't have to wait until you're dead like Jonathan Larson, the author of the musical Rent or John Kennedy Toole who committed suicide eleven years before his novel, a Confederacy of Dunces, became a massive hit. The first author died from AIDS right before his musical premiered to great success and won three Tony awards. The second killed himself before he was discovered. If he hadn't given up, like Robert E Howard who also surrendered at a young age, they would have seen the success that eluded them and perhaps created more great work.

As the movie *Galaxy Quest* reminds us, "Never give up. Never surrender."

Create and you will have created. Once you give birth to art, you become a creator and who knows what fame and fortune lies ahead.

It's really up to you. So what are you waiting for?

USEFUL WEB LINKS

The best writing software on the market right now is *Scrivener*, which as of this writing is only $40. It is an extremely powerful word processing software for writers that will export you manuscript to any format, let you map out scenes in cork board mode, add research to your project references including images and video. And it lets you format your book for various ebook formats as well as others. It also has templates for comic book scripts, screenplays, teleplays, etc, Truly a great program. I also recommend their software Scrapple.

    literatureandlatte.com

TV Tropes is a website devoted to all the writing conventions and tricks found in fiction, not just TV. They cover movies, comics and the like. There's a lot more discussed on that site than I covered in this book. It's worth a good read.

    tvtropes.org

Save the Cat is a website created by the late Blake Snyder and is maintained by people who have advanced his theories of writing screenplays. He wrote a book of the same name which is excellent and talks in much more detail about the log line.

    savethecat.com

The Author Marketing Club will provide tools and how to videos to help you market your books. It's a very useful service with some great tools.

    authormarketingclub.com

Writers.Net is a resource for writers, editors and

publishers to find each other and talk shop.

writers.net

Smashwords is a ebook publishing and distribution site that will publish your work to hundreds of ebook sellers. They also have helpful free books that will help you with marketing and formatting.

smashwords.com

Amazon is the largest ebook seller and also has a fulfillment house called Createspace where you can print your books. Amazon has helped lead the revolution making publishing easy for everyone.

amazon.com

createspace.com

ABOUT THE AUTHOR

James Hudnall broke into the comics scene in 1986 with his comic Espers, which was illustrated by V for Vendetta artist David Lloyd. He went on to work for Marvel, DC, Image and Malibu and others. He was one of the early adapters of Manga in the US for Viz Comics and also worked on Hong Kong comics. His comic Harsh Realm inspired a TV show on Fox, and many of his comics projects are in development in Hollywood.

In addition to writing James has worked as a producer, a political writer and an Internet engineer. He currently lives in San Diego, California.

Many of his comics and books are available at on line sellers.

www.ingramcontent.com/pod-product-compliance
Lightning Source LLC
Chambersburg PA
CBHW071333280526
45787CB00001B/86